Getting Connected, Staying Connected

Getting Connected, Staying Connected

Loving One Another, Day by Day

A very practical, step-by-step guidebook for couples
and their families

John DeFrain
Extension Family and Community
Development Specialist at the University of
Nebraska–Lincoln, and the UNL Extension
Family Research and Writing Team

iUniverse, Inc.
Bloomington

Getting Connected, Staying Connected
Loving One Another, Day by Day

University of Nebraska–Lincoln Extension helps people put knowledge to work. It provides a wide range of educational opportunities, delivered in a variety of venues, so participants have knowledge they can use to make sound decisions to better their lives. Extension educators and specialists teach, facilitate, and collaborate in providing research-based information to Nebraskans. For more information about University of Nebraska–Lincoln Extension, visit the website, www.extension.unl. edu. For more information about the UNL for Families Extension Team, visit www.unlforfamilies. unl.edu.

Extension is a Division of the Institute of Agriculture and Natural Resources at the University of Nebraska–Lincoln cooperating with the Counties and the United States Department of Agriculture.

University of Nebraska–Lincoln Extension educational programs abide with the nondiscrimination policies of the University of Nebraska–Lincoln and the United States Department of Agriculture.

iUniverse books may be ordered through booksellers or by contacting:

iUniverse
1663 Liberty Drive
Bloomington, IN 47403
www.iuniverse.com
1-800-Authors (1-800-288-4677)

ISBN: 978-1-4697-6358-3 (sc)
ISBN: 978-1-4697-6359-0 (hc)
ISBN: 978-1-4697-6360-6 (ebk)

Printed in the United States of America

iUniverse rev. date: 06/19/2012

Research and Writing Team:

John DeFrain
Gail Brand
Maureen Burson
Ann Fenton
Jeanette Friesen
Janet Hanna
Mary Nelson
Cindy Strasheim
Dianne Swanson
LaDonna Werth

Contributors:

Kathleen Lodl
Beth Birnstihl

Dedication

This book about strong couple and family relationships is dedicated to our loving partners and our wonderful families

CONTENTS

CHAPTER 1

Introduction: The World Couples and Families Live In Today

The Truth About Marriage and Family

Couples and families have it in their power to be happy with each other and create a pleasant and peaceful home environment in which they live together.

Our aim in writing about *getting connected and staying connected* is to accentuate the positive—to show clearly and simply how happy couple and family relationships are created and maintained over time. We will be continuously demonstrating *what works well* in creating strong, enduring relationships. The constant focus will be on how human beings get connected with each other on an intimate level, and how we stay connected with each other through the years. Since no couple or family on earth is perfectly happy, perfectly stable, perfectly functioning together in life, we have chosen to write a book that will be useful to everyone: not only those with lots of challenges but those with just a few challenges. Every couple and family has difficulties in life. The key is how well they can work together to deal positively and effectively with these challenges.

So, then, what is the truth about marriage and family today? How are families doing? Researchers do not have the ability (or the invitation) to go behind closed doors and, like the proverbial fly on the wall, to observe what is going on in all the couple and family relationships around the world. However, researchers specializing in the understanding of couple and family relationships on a global level are continuously striving to develop a better picture of what is happening today. The best information available indicates that, in general, couples and families are doing reasonably well. The average couple and family in many cultures tell us

1

they are relatively happy with each other and highly value their families. Yes, there are many couples who are in the process of breaking up or melting down; and, yes, there are many families in the midst of violence, despair and disorganization. But the best estimates researchers can make with the research technologies available today lead us to estimate that *most* couples and families *most of the time* are doing okay.

Is okay good enough? Is there room for improvement? Of course. No question about that. All couples and all families have many things they could do to improve the quality of their lives together and increase the happiness and the love they feel for each other. That's what motivates us to write this book and contribute in a modest way to the general well-being.

Is there reason for despair? Yes, there are also countless situations couples and families face that are notoriously grim. To deny this reality would be foolish; to ignore it and not work to make life better for couples and families would be irresponsible. But the fact remains that for many couples and families, there is significant reason for thanksgiving, and the strengths they regularly demonstrate in their relationships with each other are remarkable.

Defining *Happy Couples, Strong Families,* and *Love*

Discussions of couple and family issues often begin with definitions of terms used. Since our focus in this book is on positive, loving relationships among couples and families, we take an inclusive view emphasizing the quality of the relationships involved rather than legal definitions and blood ties. From this way of looking at things, the strength of the relationship is of utmost interest and importance. For example, two-parent families are often assumed to be superior to single-parent families. But in the real world, there are many two-parent families torn by violence, emotional and sexual abuse, alcoholism and a host of other problems. As one single parent explained to us, "My children and I are much, much happier now that we are safe and free from my ex-husband's violent temper and drunken rage." Similarly, there are many stepfamilies who are doing very well in the world today, regardless of the negative stereotypes people often have of stepfamilies. Also, countless extended families of many shapes and sizes are healthy places for people to live. And many families with gay and lesbian members have very loving relationships, in spite of the prejudice they may face. Indeed, families come in many different shapes and sizes. In our recent study of strong families in Australia, we asked family members to describe the type of family they lived in—the structure of their family. The family members described, literally, 32 different types of strong families. Not just one type, for example, Mom, Dad and the kids. But 32 different types. And because there are so many different structures for strong families, it is most important to focus on the quality of the relationships inside these families. By looking at family relationships—actual behavior—rather than structures, you learn a great deal about what is happening in the home.

What, then, is a happy couple? A strong family? A successful family? We believe the answer lies in the *strengths* of the relationship rather than the structure of the family. Here are the qualities we are looking for when we assess the strength of a couple's relationship or the strength of a family. These strengths have emerged from research at the University of Nebraska–Lincoln and allied institutions over the past 35 years involving 27,000 family members in 38 countries around the world:

- *Appreciation and affection for each other*. Genuinely felt, and expressed regularly.
- *Commitment to the family*. Work and other priorities are not allowed to take too much time away from family interaction. The family is highly valued by its members, and individuals are faithful to each other.
- *Positive communication*. Family members enjoy talking with each other and listening to each other. The interactions are open, honest, straightforward and pleasant.
- *Enjoyable time together*. Similarly, family members like to be with each other and spend a considerable amount of time enjoying each other's company. They are good friends.
- *Spiritual well-being and shared values*. Family members share a sense of hope, optimism, faith, safety and happiness together. Their home is a sanctuary and their relationships bring them comfort. Spiritual well-being can be seen as the caring center within each individual that promotes sharing, love and compassion.
- *The ability to manage stress and crisis effectively*. Strong families are not immune to troubles in life, but they know how to work through hard times *together* rather than exploding and blaming each other when difficulties arise. The question *is not*, "Who's

responsible for this happening?" The question *is*, "Where do we go from here?"

The six strengths are not independent of each other but are all closely related to each other. *Appreciation and affection* make *positive communication* happen; *commitment to the family* makes it easier to *manage stress and crisis effectively*, *spending enjoyable time together* contributes to a sense of *spiritual well-being and shared values*, and so forth. The six qualities are so closely related to each other, in fact, that it's possible to think about one major couple and family strength that embodies all the rest: a feeling of positive *emotional connection with each other*.

The six major qualities of strong families, as outlined over the years by the research on family strengths, can be seen as a very useful working definition of *love* in a family. Love is both a feeling we have for each other and a series of positive behaviors that we express toward each other. Thus, our appreciation and affection for each other, our commitment, our positive communication, enjoyable time together, sense of spiritual well-being and shared values when we are together, and our ability to work through difficulties together—all of these behaviors toward each other are demonstrations of love for each other, and when we act in these positive ways toward each other, we are likely to have loving feelings toward each other.

Is this a high bar? Is it difficult to create happiness together as a couple? Difficult to create relationship strengths as a family? Difficult to find a way to genuinely love each other and see this love endure over time?

Yes, it *is* difficult! However, to create a positive, long-term relationship does *not* need to be viewed as drudgery. Instead, the effort we invest will help reach the goal of a loving and caring relationship—one of the greatest gifts we will ever receive. The effort should not be seen negatively, but in a positive manner, for the goal is a strong, healthy relationship. Think about it: Is it drudgery to express appreciation and affection for each other? Is it drudgery to find ways to have enjoyable time with each other?

The goal should be to live our lives in a way in which we find the time to create special and intimate moments with each other. If we have the good sense to be able to do that, everything else will likely fall into place. Often, in our highly competitive and materialistic society, we lose sight of the fact that positive, loving relationships are the greatest gifts we have.

Challenges Couples and Families Face in Our Society

Life has never been easy, and as David H. Olson says, "All the problems in the world either begin in families or end up in families." Olson, a family researcher and family therapist, argues that families can create their own problems. For example, if the family members choose to be argumentative and violent with each other, this brings on a host of difficulties for them of their own making. Other problems families create for themselves would include alcohol problems related to the decision to drink; health problems caused by the decision to smoke; relationship problems caused by the decision to have a lover outside marriage, and so forth. For these kinds of difficulties, the family has to find ways of dealing with the problems it has created by unwise decisions.

The rest of the problems families face, in Olson's view, are problems the family did not create but were thrust upon the family by the outside world. For example, war. An individual family does not cause a nation to go to war, but individual families are forced to deal with the consequences of war on a daily basis: where to live when the family's home is destroyed; how to survive when a breadwinner is killed; how to find the resources to care for injured family members and family members suffering from ill health due to diseases caused by the collapse of a country's public health system, and so forth.

Olson would agree that assessing responsibility for a family's problems is difficult. Yes, a family member dying of lung cancer related to smoking *chose* to smoke, but responsibility should be shared by tobacco companies who aggressively target young, impressionable individuals to begin using an addictive drug at an early age to get them hooked. Similarly, when a country goes to war, everyone in the country shares some responsibility for the drift toward war, even though the final decision was made by the country's leaders. When we jump on a bandwagon, we should share some of the consequences. Assessing responsibility is a difficult thing to do. Olson's point is still well taken: All the problems in the world end up with families being responsible to find solutions for the problems they face.

And, the social environment in which we live today is rife with problems. Family specialists David H. Olson, John DeFrain and Linda Skogrand outline 10 major challenges families face today:

- *Stress, change, and materialism.* Competition, technology, and the drive to acquire material things have all combined to create a stressful environment for many people in our country today.
- *Lack of time for oneself and significant others.* In an overly-busy social environment in which individuals often seem to pride themselves on how hard they are working, we lose sight of our own personal needs and the importance of spending enjoyable and meaningful time with loved ones and friends.
- *Increasing use of child care outside the family.* In the rush we sometimes force young children into child care settings for long hours. Many parents argue quite persuasively, of course, that child care outside the home is essential, especially for low-income families struggling to keep their head above water. Many other parents believe, also quite sincerely, that long hours in group care settings can be stressful for young children, and that as parents they are missing the joy of seeing their children grow.
- *Instability of couple and family relationships.* Our fast-paced social environment, focusing on competitive achievement and the acquisition of material things contributes to a culture of divorce, in which marital breakdown is common. There is no question that many marriages are fractured by severe problems that are probably insurmountable—emotional, physical, and sexual abuse in families come to mind, along with the abuse of alcohol and other drugs. But other marriages disintegrate for more insidious reasons: lack of time invested in each other; lack of creative and careful nurturance of each other; an emotional or physical affair in which a partner searches for the perfect mate outside the marriage and the excitement of romantic love, even though a happy and romantic relationship can be created with the current partner; an affair with one's work or an affair with one's church or mosque or synagogue. The list of ways marriages fall apart is probably endless.
- *Violence, criminal victimization, and fear.* Violent and abusive behaviors are major causes of death, injury, stress and fear in American society. Crime victimizes millions annually. Suicide takes the lives of nearly 30,000 Americans a year. More than 900,000 children are victims of abuse and neglect each year.

- *Use of alcohol, tobacco, and other drugs.* More deaths and disabilities can be attributed to substance abuse in the United States than any other cause. Approximately 18 million Americans have alcohol problems, and 5 to 6 million more have other drug problems. More than half of all American adults have a family history of alcoholism or problem drinking, and more than 9 million children live with a parent who is dependent on alcohol and/or illicit drugs. Alcohol contributes to the death of about 85,000 people in the U.S. each year, and 435,000 die from smoking tobacco, chewing tobacco, and breathing other people's smoke.

- *The Internet and human relationships.* The Internet has become an amazing tool for use by millions of Americans, and the benefits are undeniable. There are, however, negative consequences of the development of this technology, including the exposure of children to unwanted sexual solicitations. And, researchers have found that increased Internet use can result in decreased communication with other family members, causing a decline in psychological well-being.

- *Changing gender roles and the balance of power in families.* More adequate birth control methods, relative affluence and access to higher education, and opportunities for working outside the home and having their own money have all combined to shift the balance of power in families, giving women more say in how their lives unfold. These changes have been stressful for many men. But many other men have seen them as golden opportunities for focusing less on job/career responsibilities because their partner is also a breadwinner. Men who take a more contemporary view of gender roles and the balance of power in families focus more on the satisfaction of seeing their children grow, and enjoying the opportunity for an even more intimate and understanding relationship with their spouse.

- *Urban migration and overcrowding.* According to the U.S. Census Bureau, approximately 79% of Americans are urban dwellers, while rural Americans make up 21% of the population. Two enduring and competing beliefs throughout much of American history are that *economic opportunity lies in the city* and that *the peaceful and satisfying life lies close to the land in the country.* With the advance of agricultural and industrial technology, cities have

7

grown explosively in population, while rural areas have steadily emptied out in many places. Fewer people are able to farm more and more acres, and rural communities dwindle in size. The problem of where to live falls to the family to decide, of course, and this decision can be wrenching, especially when some choose to stay in their small community and some choose to go to the city. Families are divided and don't get to see each other as much as they would like.

- *Financial problems and the global economy.* Money troubles are the most common problems couples and families face, regardless of how much money they might make. While many Americans are financially secure today, many others live close to the edge. According to the U.S. Census Bureau, 4 in 10 of all poor people are children. Global competition compounds these difficulties for families as they watch jobs being lost to other countries, as factories close and other industries outsource work around the world.

Advantages of a Sound Marriage

If it is true that all the problems in the world either begin or end up in families, the importance of the family as an instrument of safety, stability and comfort for individuals becomes undeniable. The family becomes, in the proverbial sense, the haven that we all seek in a heartless world. And, the foundation of many families is a strong marriage. If the couple relationship is in danger, the whole family faces difficulties.

Sociologist Linda Waite argues that marriage can be good for a person's physical and mental health, good for financial stability, good for one's sex life, and good for one's children. Like exercising and eating right, getting married is another step toward living longer and better.

Waite argues that married people live longer than unmarried or divorced people; that they are happier than single, widowed, or cohabiting people; that they are more successful in their careers, earn more, and have more wealth; married women experience less domestic abuse; married people report that they have sex more frequently and their sexual relationships are more satisfying physically and emotionally than singles; and that children generally fare better emotionally, socially and financially in families in which their parents are married.

Waite explains that the situation is similar to a program of exercise. "Studies show that, on average, people who exercise experience health benefits. The next step is to say that you should exercise." In a similar vein, she argues that "a consistent body of work suggests to me that an okay marriage, one that isn't terrible, causes improvements" in a person's general well-being. Marriage, she believes, can be not only a sign of a longer, healthier life, higher income, and better sex, but she also sees it as a cause of these good things.

Why would this be so? In a strong marriage the partners value and cherish each other. They care for, counsel, nurture, encourage and love each other, helping their partner through life's most difficult times and enjoying countless good times together. These innumerable little gifts partners bestow on each other lead to a better and more confident attitude toward life, the belief that one can succeed in her or his efforts.

Of course, this does not mean that if you are single and run out today and get married your life will automatically improve. If life were only that simple. But it does mean that for many people who find a good partner, and who are skillful and lucky enough to be able to create a sound marriage, life can be quite satisfying.

Thus, our focus here will steadfastly remain on how to create and maintain a sound relationship. In essence, how to get connected and how to stay connected.

Very Short Stories from Real People

> Before we had children, Rotary Club was an important part of my life. It was my way to contribute to the community. My husband knew that the relationships were important to me. He arranged his work schedule so he could be home on Tuesday to care for the children, so I could continue to participate in the 7:30 a.m. weekly meetings. His support provided me the opportunity to serve as president.

> When we first had children, we kept saying that we have to find time together. Until the children were two, we really weren't able to carve out couple time. At that point in our

life, we re-focused our couple time together. We sometimes have a niece watch our children so we can get a cup of coffee together.

The everyday rituals such as a kiss good morning, a kiss goodbye, a good night hug are the most meaningful. Mealtimes are the things that sustain us. We work very hard to eat together each day.

We both came from small farming communities and met at college. We got married and went into professional careers. Both of us miss the closeness of family and the different lifestyle of the rural area compared to the city. Though we have friendships at work, we are facing a difficult transition. We no longer feel we fit in comfortably at home when we visit. But at the same time, we're not completely comfortable with life in the fast lane. The thing we have is that we understand each other and are each other's best friend.

Discussion Questions

1. If you would like to become a parent, describe the parent you want to become.
2. Describe in detail where you would ideally like to live (the location, the state, house size, rural area, urban area, suburban).
3. If you had only 24 hours left to live, how would you spend your time?
4. In the last week, when and where have you and your partner communicated the most and the best? What can you learn from this?
5. How would you describe the breadwinner of a household? Does that influence the division of duties in the household?
6. How do real-life relationships differ from the romantic expectations of television and movie relationships?

Tips for Strengthening Your Relationship

1. Marry your best friend.
2. Find a partner you can give unconditional love to and receive unconditional love from.
3. Somehow, every day, let your partner know specific things that you appreciate about her/him.
4. Somehow, every day, take time to nurture your couple relationship, just the two of you.

CHAPTER 2

Families Across the Lifespan: The Normal, To-Be-Expected Satisfactions and Challenges Couples and Families Experience

Family researchers and theorists today discuss stage theories of life, focusing on *the stages of family development*. Depending on the scholar, there are between four and 24 different stages in the family life cycle.

We will focus here on the work of Evelyn Duvall, a major contributor to family development theory. Family development theory as it stands today looks at how couples and family members deal with various roles and developmental tasks within the marriage and the family as they move through various stages of the life cycle.

As you are well aware, couples and families are amazingly diverse and the world of families is constantly changing and evolving. For these reasons, it is probably impossible to construct a family development theory that takes into account all these important differences. However, for our purposes here, we will use Duvall's framework as a way of organizing our discussion about families across the lifespan. You can personalize this family development theory. Think about how you would adapt the general theory to fit in where you are now personally as a couple and as a family.

Duvall outlined eight major stages and eight family development tasks, as shown in Table 2-1.

Table 2.1 The Traditional Family Life Cycle Stages and Developmental Tasks

Stages of the Family Life Cycle	Positions in the Family	Family Developmental Tasks
Stage 1. The married couple	Wife Husband	Establishing a mutually satisfying marriage Adjusting to pregnancy Fitting into the kin network
Stage 2. Childbearing	Wife / mother Husband / father Infant(s)	Having and adjusting to an infant Establishing a satisfying home for parents and infant(s)
Stage 3. Preschool-aged children	Wife / mother Husband / father Daughter / sister Son / brother	Adapting to the needs of preschool children Coping with energy depletion and lack of privacy as parents
Stage 4. School-aged children	Wife / mother Husband / father Daughter / sister Son / brother	Fitting into the community Encouraging children's educational achievements

Stage 5. Teenage children	Wife / mother Husband / father Daughter / sister Son / brother	Balancing freedom with responsibility Establishing post-parental interests
Stage 6. Launching the children	Wife / mother / grandmother Husband / father / grandfather	Launching youth into adulthood Maintaining a supportive home base
Stage 7. Middle-aged parents	Wife / mother / grandmother Husband / father / grandfather	Refocusing on the marriage relationship Maintaining kin ties with older and younger generations
Stage 8. Aging family members	Widow / widower Wife / mother / grandmother Husband / father / grandfather	Coping with death and living alone Selling the family home Adjusting to retirement

Source: Adapted from "Stages and Family Development Tasks" in *Marriage and Family Development* (6th ed.) by Evelyn Mills Duvall and Brent C. Miller, 1985, New York: Harper & Row. Copyright © 1985 by Harper & Row Publishers, Inc. Reprinted by permission of Addison-Wesley Educational Publishers, Inc.

Using Duvall's traditional framework as a springboard for our discussion, we will now look at very common satisfactions and challenges couples experience today in contemporary society as they go through the adventure of life together. We will construct this discussion simply by recounting stories husbands and wives have told us over the years. You will readily see the many different ways people talk about being a couple.

As you read this discussion of the various periods of couple and family life, think about your own experience and the experiences of other family members.

Stage 1. The Married Couple

Establishing a mutually satisfying marriage

> We had lived together several years before we got married, so we understood each other pretty well. I knew what to expect and he knew what to expect. The roughest times were before we were married, when we were living together. That was the most difficult adjustment.

> We would not have ever even thought about living together before marriage. Besides, my father and her father would have killed me if I wanted to do that. So, I lived at home with my parents and she lived at home with her parents, and then we got married and moved in with each other. Though we had dated a long time before we got married, it was a big adjustment for both of us. Dating on Friday and Saturday night is not the same as living together day after day after day.

> We adjusted to marriage pretty quickly. But life was always changing. We got jobs and left those jobs and got others. We moved from apartment to apartment, house to house, city to city. As the circumstances of our life together changed, we also changed as individuals. And so we had to readjust to each other and our marriage changed. Perhaps the biggest adjustment was when we decided we wanted children.

Adjusting to pregnancy

> She was pregnant when we got married. It seems like we never really had any time to adjust to each other because we were always focused on children, even during pregnancy.

> A few weeks after our wedding I started getting morning sickness. I had hoped that we would have five years together to get to know each other as a couple, then have children. That's certainly not how things worked out!

Fitting into the kin network

> She came from a huge extended family. Everyone on earth seemed to be a cousin. I came from a small family and the few relatives we had were a long way off. Getting used to all her relatives and all these birthday parties and endless get-togethers was hard for me. We always seemed to get in an argument just about the time we were leaving for yet another family gathering.

Stage 2. Childbearing

Having and adjusting to an infant

> Do I remember what our life was like before we had our first baby? Not really. Everything changed. Totally. Life was not a game anymore. It got very serious. But we liked the new responsibilities. We were mature and ready.

> We didn't have a clue about what we were getting into. We hadn't planned for this. It just happened. And then here we were: parents. Every day was a learning experience. Every day was an adventure. We had no clue how clueless we were.

The pregnancy went really well, up until the last week. I woke up one morning and didn't notice any movement. I went into the doctor that afternoon and after examining me she looked terribly startled, then sad. My baby had died. Four days later in the hospital I delivered a dead baby. We never did find out what happened. She was a perfect little baby in every way. She just wasn't alive. I don't know what I would have done without Jason. He was really the only person on earth who understood how terrible our loss was to us. Without him, I might have died, also.

Establishing a satisfying home for parents and infant(s)

Since we were in our mid-thirties we had developed a very organized approach to life after being together for several years. We tried to apply this ultra-organized approach to babies just like we did everything else in life. Babies, however, don't follow their parents' plans. Our baby took three years to conceive because of all kinds of health complications. I had surgery. When nothing happened we considered adoption and looked into that. It seemed terribly expensive and we didn't have lots of money. Finally, we found a more affordable approach—we laughed and called it the paper cup and turkey baster method. The clinic only charged about $1,000. It worked, the first try. But the worries through the pregnancy were endless and the trips to the specialists went on and on. Would she survive? Well, she did, of course, and now she's 7 years old and we are delighted. But we learned how planning and organization don't always work very well when you're talking about becoming parents.

It took quite awhile for me to get interested in sex again. I hadn't healed from the delivery and I was tired all the time.

———◆———

Our little boy changed every day. I didn't want to miss anything, so I spent countless hours with him. Just when I thought I had him figured out, he would change again and I had to refigure how to deal with him. What a wonderful challenge it all proved for me!

Stage 3. Preschool-Aged Children

Adapting to the needs of preschool children

For some reason I got it in my head that the minute we got Lindy potty trained that our job as parents would be pretty much done. Everything would be easy after we got through the smelly diapers. Not so!

———◆———

We had our children when we were young. There are considerable disadvantages to that, of course. You don't know what you are doing. You don't know who you are. You haven't really established yourself as an individual and as a couple. You don't have any money. But, I see couples having children in their 30s and 40s and even becoming a dad after age 50 and I think, "How do they possibly have all the energy they need to chase kids around all day?

———◆———

Coping with energy depletion and lack of privacy as parents

We were making love one night, about an hour after we got Cole in bed. We were getting really intimate. I happened to look down at the end of the bed and there were these two little eyes, open wide, peering at us in the semi-darkness: "Daddy, what are you doing?"

"Hi, Cole!" I said while Cindy covered up really fast. I whisked him up in my arms and carried him back to his room and popped him back in his crib. Cole is 20 now and he hasn't ever mentioned what he remembers from that night.

I don't think she had been out of my sight 10 seconds, but she made it from the front door of the house to the kitchen and then fell head-over-heels down the basement stairs, hitting her head very hard on the basement concrete floor. She had a huge bump on her forehead. At the ER the nurses checked her over very carefully, pronounced her okay, and looked at me suspiciously to see if I were an abusive mother. No, I wasn't abusive. I just couldn't keep up with a toddler sometimes. It was really scary.

Stage 4. School-Aged Children

Fitting into the community

We have four children and they are all special children. David is extra-special. He has a behavioral disability and is different from other kids. He's louder and somewhat odd and he just doesn't quite fit in. To protect him, I volunteered regularly in his classroom at school so the teachers would get to know and understand his needs better and the other children would see he was basically a good kid but just different. It was terribly stressful in many ways but it has turned into a career for me now. I just graduated from the University of New Mexico in special education. Years ago when I first started out in college I wanted to be an artist. How about that?

Before she went in for surgery when she was five years old, we knew she was worried. She had told her older sister that she wouldn't be going to first grade in the fall because she would be dead. It was clearly time to sit down with her and talk with her about the surgery. I explained what was going to happen and why it was important for her to have the surgery. "If you don't have this done tomorrow, you could die," I told her. "Your doctor is a very good doctor and he says that you will be fine."

"But some kids die during surgery, don't they, Dad?" she asked me.

"Yes, this does happen sometimes. But we think you will be fine . . . By the way, what do you think happens when you die?"

"I'm not sure, Dad, because I have never died. But I think it's kind of like going to sleep forever and you never wake up."

"I'm not sure what happens either, Erin, but I think you're right. I think a person just goes to sleep forever and never wakes up. And that doesn't sound so bad to me, actually."

"Me neither, Dad."

That was the most difficult conversation I ever had with our daughter.

———◈———

You've been trying to be so responsible and trying so hard to do the right thing. And now you have to let them go into the world and hope that there are other good people who will care for them and love them just even a tiny bit as much as you have.

Encouraging children's educational achievements

It's such an amazing milestone when they go to school for the first time. It's the day you've been waiting for. An end to round-the-clock, 365-days-a-year child care. A breather!

And yet, it then hits you: "So, what do I do with my life now? I can't do anything. I'm just a momma."

You've been protecting them from the world. Protecting them from bullies and barking dogs and cars and TV violence and junk food. On and on and on . . . you've been protecting them. And suddenly, you leave them off at the classroom door and say, "Please God, take care of my babies."

They've gotten crazy in our state about school achievement. It's so competitive and so relentless. Homework for first graders? But they send stuff home all the time from school and so we spend a lot of time working with Ellen on her homework. I try to tell myself that it's helping create a bond with our child, but I also can't help feel that I'm conspiring with the school system to rob our daughter of some of her childhood. And it infringes on fun family activities, forcing us to sit down and do math problems when we want to take a walk in the park together. It's hard to know how to deal with all this.

Stage 5. Teenage Children

Balancing freedom with responsibility

The kids were all in countless activities in middle school and high school. It was really kind of nuts, but they had all kinds of energy and in a lot of ways it was better than having them

21

banging around the house all the time. However, it seemed as if our lives as parents were reduced to going to work and driving in the kids' carpools.

We went through a difficult period, I call it the Time of Expensive Shoes. Every time Sarah took the girls shopping they wanted the most expensive shoes imaginable, the designer brands, so they would fit in with all the other girls in school.

Finally, we figured out a way to change the rules of the game. Instead of a battle between the parents' money and the kids' desires, we decided to turn the tables on them. We gave each daughter her own stipend—stipend sounded more sophisticated than allowance. With this money they were expected to pay for school lunches, pay for entertainment and incidentals, and pay for their clothes.

They received their stipend at the beginning of the month, just like my paycheck. If they chose to blow the whole wad on a pair of shoes, that was their choice. But, they wouldn't have a penny until the next month began.

The stipend was not ungenerous, really. It was quite adequate for their needs and they never complained or begged for more money. I think it kind of surprised them how expensive they really were to their parents when you totaled it up and gave it out in one monthly sum.

And, they quickly learned that you can find really cool shoes in great shape at Goodwill for a fraction of the price at the mall.

We were pretty open about sex, I think. We always answered the kids' questions and we brought sexual issues up regularly at the dinner table. When sex was in the news, when sex was a subject of political discussion, when there was a sex scene in the movies, when they talked about a friend who was wondering if she was gay, whatever . . .

Establishing post-parental interests

So, Billy got his driver's license. I didn't have to take him to piano lessons and track and debate and everything else all the time. I got to stay at home and worry if he would make it back alive from his adventure behind the wheel.

As I think back, the teenage years were a time of transition for all of us in the family. The kids were trying to establish themselves in the world outside our home, and toward the end of this time Sharon and I were puzzling over what would come next when the parade came to an end. It was an exciting time, a frustrating time in many ways, a good time in life.

Stage 6. Launching the Children

Launching youth into adulthood

Once he found a job after high school, he rented an apartment with five other boys—a horrible dump of a place that they all loved—and we rarely saw him again for several years. Until the Sunday afternoon he brought home a beautiful girl who seemed as if she had the ability to tame him. We looked at each other when they went out the door and said, "Yes."

***

They didn't all go at once. It was gradual and that helped. The noise and hubbub just kind of died down gradually, in three steps. The first departure, actually, was pretty neat for everybody. It was a new experience. Ellen was finishing up college and, amazingly, she found a job right away at a school in Tennessee. We all helped her move down there and her mom and I felt good that one little bird was launched, but fortunately we still had two in the nest to keep us busy for a while.

***

Raising our kids successfully was the most important and meaningful thing we did together as a couple. It brought countless satisfactions and bonded us closely as a couple.

Would we like to start over and do it again now? Are you crazy? We have turned that page to a new chapter in our life together.

Maintaining a supportive home base

When the last one left—we stood in the doorway of her empty room and talked in almost a whisper. It was really very sad. I figured out that we had children in our home for 29 years. And then suddenly, it was all over. Her sister came to help her move out and all that was left were a few dust bunnies in the corners and smudge marks on the walls. We stood in the doorway of the room and talked softly. Our voices seemed to echo across the small, empty room.

For four months I hated it. I was used to commotion, to life, to youth and energy and now the house seemed too big.

Then, I crossed some kind of emotional threshold. After four months I began to enjoy the solitude. The freedom of going somewhere anytime we wished and not having to make all kinds of arrangements in regard to kids. The freedom and the quiet were compelling. Should we get a dog? Nope. We don't want to have to take care of anyone for a while. It felt marvelously selfish.

And when the kids would come home on occasion for a brief visit, it was okay for a while but they brought their barking dogs and noisy friends and the TV was back blasting away with those awful reality programs. After a couple hours we were delighted they had come to visit and we were delighted when it was time for them to drive off back to their own lives.

We've got many friends whose kids came home again for a while, for one reason or another. We didn't think it would happen to us, but when she left her husband who was drinking and chasing around, we knew she didn't have a penny and didn't have anywhere to go. And we loved our grandson and knew it wouldn't last forever.

Sometimes it felt like forever though, because it took her over a year to find a decent job. And her husband had hid a lot of debts from her that surfaced after the separation. She got stuck with a big chunk of his bills.

But she finally got back on her feet and when she and Chad moved out we were genuinely sad to see them go and happy that we rose to the occasion.

Stage 7. Middle-Aged Parents

Refocusing on the marriage relationship

All of a sudden we had time for each other again. We were a couple. It had been so long ago when we had some privacy and a bit of extra money and time for each other. The phone wasn't always ringing off the hook for the kids. We started to get to know each other after being separated by life for so many years. It has been wonderful.

———◆◆◆———

Do you know what it's like to find your sex life again at age 48?

———◆◆◆———

I know people sometimes talk about empty-nest syndrome and the sadness and loss parents can feel when their children leave home. We had some of that, of course, but the major emotion I think we felt was relief. A long race had ended and we were satisfied with the result.

———◆◆◆———

We stayed together for several years, even though the marriage had died. We did this for the kids, I guess, though I don't know what *for the kids* really means anymore. The kids knew the marriage was dead, too, so what were we trying to hide?

It's funny. Now that we're divorced, we're good friends. We have dinner together when the children come home, and we go for walks around the lake on occasion to catch up on news. We're still parents of our children, so we need to talk.

Will we ever get back together? No, I don't want that. But I do enjoy his companionship on occasion.

Maintaining kin ties with older and younger generations

I've read about the so-called sandwiched generation, the middle-aged people who are caught in between their young adult children and their aging parents. We focused on our two children until they left home and got established in the world. And then, not long after that job was done, our mothers started to fail. Their health started to go downhill and, looking back, this turned into a six-year-long downward spiral that also wore us down tremendously. Between kid issues and parent issues, we were often frazzled.

The children have moved away from home. All of our parents are gone. In some ways it feels lonely, but all things considered, you know, it's a pretty good life. Our financial situation is as good as it has ever been and we have found that we really like each other. Our marriage is as good as it has been in a long time.

When our granddaughter was born, we saw how well our daughter and her husband cared for this new baby. It was miraculous. And we looked at each other and said, "Well, we raised our daughter to be a good mother and we probably influenced her good decision in choosing a husband. Maybe we didn't do so bad as parents after all."

Stage 8. Aging Family Members

Coping with death and living alone

> When Bill died, a part of me died with him. Society says you should have a funeral, feel sad for two weeks, and start living again. To hell with society! You don't love someone for 54 years and "get over it" immediately. My life will never be the same.

> When my father died, my mother seemed to blossom. She never drove a car—he always complained about her driving—and so at age 73 after he was gone she went to driver education classes at the local high school and got her license. Can you imagine a 73-year-old learning to drive with a car full of teenagers?

> A few years after my husband died, I met a wonderful gentleman and we began dating. It was so much fun to feel loved again. My kids said, "You're 78 years old, Mom!" And I replied, "I'm *only* 78 years old!" Finally, we could all laugh about it. I accused them of micro-managing my life and they said turnabout was fair play. They said they were just doing what I did to them when they were teenagers.

Selling the family home

> It took six months to clean out and clean up the house and another year to sell it. But we were rattling around in a four-bedroom house with the children gone and no grandchildren in sight at the moment. We bought a condo in Florida. We'll stay two years for tax purposes and maybe stay longer. Who knows? This is the first time in our life when nobody's telling us all the time what to do.

Adjusting to retirement

> I flunked retirement. That's the only way I can describe it. I quit work at 65 and stayed home with Shelley. But I got in her way—advising her how to organize her kitchen drawers, wanting her to quit her activities so she would spend all her time with me. Shelley was gracious about it all, for a while, but after two years she shooed me away. We got in three nice trips during that time and I cleaned out the garage and the basement. But that wasn't enough for me, so I went back to work part-time and found a meaningful balance in my retirement life.

—✦—

> I'm quite happy that we're now 55 years down the road together and still married to each other. The experiences we shared together, I wouldn't sell them for a million dollars. And, at the same time, I wouldn't want to go through all that again. I wouldn't want to be 19 again. No way. I'm happy being 75. She's still a babe to me, even though we still have our disagreements.

The Grand Procession of Life

Every human life is unique. We all know this. And, every family is unique. However, there are common patterns in life that many couples and families experience, and that is why family development theory today remains useful to discuss. It helps us see that we are not alone in the world—many people are facing the same challenges we are facing. There's comfort in that thought.

What, then, are the normal, to-be-expected satisfactions and challenges that many couples and families experience during the different stages of their lives together? In sum, most of us seek a long-term, satisfying relationship with a partner. Most of us will marry at some time, and most of these marriages will be at least reasonably good most of the time, though there will be inevitable ups and downs. Many people will have children. Adjusting to pregnancy will be an exciting and sometimes difficult challenge for many. And finding a way to get along with each other's extended family will be hard for many couples.

Adjusting to an infant will be a difficult task and the couple's life is likely to be changed in countless ways. Coping with depleted energy and lack of privacy will be common problems among parents of preschool-aged children. When children go to school the family begins to adapt even more to the needs and guidelines of the community. Parents will expend a good deal of energy encouraging their children's educational achievements. As the children grow into teenagers, parents will strive to help find a balance between the young person's drive for freedom and independence on the one hand, and the young person's obligations to the family and the community on the other. Most parents will rise to the many challenges they face as their children grow. When the children leave home as young adults, most will be looking forward to a new stage in life. Some adult children will return home for a time because of job loss, divorce, health reasons, and other life crises. When this happens, most parents will adapt to the return of their adult child and be supportive during the crisis. Most parents and adult children hope to maintain reasonably strong ties to each other, but with space in between to allow for individuality and growth.

For those couples who do not have children, most will find meaning in life through their partnership, their work, and their friendships. These childless couples, whether they are voluntarily childless or not, are likely to find happiness and satisfaction in life, just as those who have become parents.

The empty nest for most couples is a good time in life, a time when financial resources are more likely to be adequate. Fewer parental responsibilities give couples a chance to focus on each other again. There can be a rekindling of old romantic feelings. Couples in this time of life generally strive to maintain ties with their children. They are also likely to be even more involved with the grandparents' generation, especially when elderly family members' health begins to fail.

All good things in life come to an end. A spouse dies and the surviving partner struggles to create a new life in the face of loss and loneliness. Some widows and widowers find another partner, while others build a new way of living. Moving out of the family home, which has sheltered the family members' dreams for many years, is a significant transition in the lives of countless people. And finding new interests and activities after retirement can be both a challenge and a delight for those who have invested many years on the job and who have been defined, in many ways, by their work. The majority of individuals make the adjustment to retirement well.

Discussion Questions

1. How did your life change at each stage?
2. What were the highlights at each stage?
3. Discuss the pros and cons of consciously not having children.
4. What family traditions do you love or hate? Which ones would you change?
5. Name someone who you believe has done a great job of adjusting to retirement. Describe how it looks.
6. Americans tend to strive toward *independence*. Many other cultures put a higher priority on *interdependence*. What are the advantages of each?

Tips for Strengthening Your Relationship

1. Share the highs and lows of your day. Take a daily 5 + 5. This time can help couples connect—even for just a few minutes—with one-on-one personal conversations. Five minutes for you to share and five minutes for your partner to share. Be sure to maintain eye contact and *listen*!
2. Spend time with your family every day. Eat with your family each day or spend several minutes with each family member.
3. Enjoy life at the stage you are in. Don't spend so much time thinking and planning for tomorrow that you forget *right now*.
4. Don't micromanage your personal life like it's a job.
5. Remember to have a couple date every week. Even better, have two dates a week.
6. The first challenge for single-parent families is to see themselves as *real* families not just pieces of a family. Don't get caught in the trap of downgrading your single-parent family.
7. If TV is eliminating your communication in the family, you may want to turn it off.
8. Few dating couples would get married if they had as little focused conversation as most married couples do.

31

9. Write in your personal journal about the *Aha!* moments of your life.
10. Intergenerational experiences in your family will create positive feelings in all generations. Keep the generations in your family connected.

CHAPTER 3

You Don't Marry an Individual,
You Marry a Family

Successfully Merging Two Individuals
From Different Family Cultures to Create
Your Own *New* Family Culture

When two people meet and their attraction to each other begins to grow, the focus is usually not on their families. Instead, *he* sees her sparkling eyes and smile, her beautiful hair, her warm and accepting laugh. *She* sees his energy, his sense of humor, his ability to listen to her with his heart . . . the list lovers can generate regarding what has attracted them to their mate is, perhaps, endless. Why not make your own list right now?

And though everyone has a different list of traits and qualities that are attractive to them, early in the relationship thoughts about her family of origin or his family of origin often are not in the forefront of one's mind. We are thinking and dreaming about an individual, not the whole clan.

Some family therapists will be quick to point out, however, that in an important sense, individuality is somewhat of an illusion. As the late Dr. Carl Whitaker was fond of saying, "There is no such thing as an individual in the world. We are only fragments of families." Whitaker meant that human beings are so inextricably interwoven into the fabric of their families that it is difficult to really separate them out apart from each other. We are so connected to each other in families that in a genuine sense, whatever happens to one member of a family is really happening to everyone else in the family, also.

So, even though we don't often think about our beloved's family of origin early in the relationship, as the couple spends more and more time together and gets to know each other better, the family of origin inevitably comes into the picture. Some individuals don't take their partner home "to meet the family" until the pair is getting relatively serious about the relationship, partially because of fear that parents, sisters, brothers, grandparents and others won't be very accepting and welcoming, sometimes because of fear that the prospective mate will think the family is nuts.

When the relationship has blossomed and talk of long-term commitment has surfaced, the family of origin looms larger in the minds of the couple, and the partners quickly learn, as the old saying goes, that, "You don't marry an individual, you marry a family". You marry into a family culture that may be quite different from the family culture from which you came. And today as the world becomes smaller and smaller, it is becoming more likely that you will be marrying into a community that you did not grow up in, and even an ethnic or national-level culture that you really know little about. Think in depth about the lives of your many friends and relatives: Did they fall in love with the girl next door? The boy from South Carolina? The girl from New York or Romania or China? How diverse has the world in which you live become? One woman we know who lives in a very small town deep in the Great Plains has two wonderful daughters-in-law, one from Russia and one from Trinidad. Who would have thought that her two very rural boys would marry internationally? But these new young ladies bring something new and special to small town life.

Our focus here will be on mate selection: how we pick a mate, how we successfully merge two individuals from different family cultures, and how we inevitably create a new couple and family culture that works well for this wonderful new relationship bound together by feelings of love and caring for each other. It's not just a matter of adopting the cultural values, behaviors and rules of her family or his family, with her family's approach to living winning out over his family's approach, or vice versa. Individuals often try to force their partner into adopting all the cultural values of the family in which they grew up in, but this can be very damaging to the marriage. One partner cannot "win" while one "loses," for ultimately the partnership loses.

Instead, it's a matter of creating a new culture that fits the values and needs of the couple as they join together. In the final analysis, some cultural values, behaviors and rules will stay the same because the partners are in general agreement about them; and, inevitably, some new cultural values, behaviors and rules will have to be created by the couple if they are to succeed in their new relationship. Sometimes the couple has to choose a new path together if the relationship is to survive, and this choice may be in direct conflict with members of their families of origin.

How do couples deal with the inevitable guilt, frustration and fear that often goes with the conflict they find themselves in with their families of origin? This certainly is not an easy issue to resolve, and the differences often can last a lifetime without any clear resolution. But in the final analysis, the new couple represents the future and if they are to survive as a couple, they need to have the *courage* and *strength* to decide what is best for them and then let their families of origin know that they will stand together by their decision. No one ever said marriage was easy.

In the final analysis, this process is all a matter of adjustment: We dream for a partner who has everything we want and nothing we don't want. In reality, we find a partner who has many things we want, and brings along other things that may prove startling, less appealing, or cause us considerable discomfort and even pain. We begin the process of adjustment, which lasts as long as the relationship lasts, and in reality is a never-ending process of learning to love each other in spite of the traits and qualities that may cause us to bristle or gasp on occasion.

If the cultural conflicts are too great and the pair finds it impossible to resolve them, the relationship is quite likely to be unhappy and the pair will have a difficult time staying together. If the differences are manageable, the pair is likely to forge a strong and loving bond.

The search, if we are to be realistic in our thinking, is not for the perfect mate. The search is for a very good friend and partner to share life's ups and downs; someone who is on our side, someone who will be there in times of need, someone we can depend on.

Human Beings Tend to Be Attracted to Potential Partners with Similar Characteristics

How do I choose a mate? What am I looking for? What are the important characteristics of the person that will give me a good chance of building a strong relationship? Family researchers have been trying to understand how people choose partners for a long time. Two broad, separate lines of thinking stand out when one reads the professional literature over the past 50 years. These approaches can be put quite simply and succinctly: *birds of a feather flock together* and *opposites attract*. Let's look closer:

Birds of a feather flock together. Individuals tend to marry someone much like themselves: someone of the same ethnic group, educational level, socioeconomic status, religion, and values. Of course, many people cross these boundary lines every day in their choices of a mate, but for most people there is a sense of comfort and familiarity in finding one who is similar to themselves in important ways. This approach to mate selection is called *homogamy*, the notion that couples often are very much alike.

Opposites attract. The second important line of thinking on mate selection has focused on the notion that people are attracted to those whose personalities and characteristics are very different from their own. Robert Winch called this approach *complementary needs theory*, because it argues that opposites can be attractive to each other. For example, a sheltered and shy young woman from a small town may be attracted to a brash and outspoken older man from the big city. She seeks more excitement in life. Her need complements his need: he fears that his drinking and daring ways may be his undoing, and seeks the shelter of a more calm, stable, and sensible partner.

Generally speaking, researchers have demonstrated that long-term marital stability is enhanced by marrying someone who is similar, especially in those areas of genuine importance to the individuals. It may be true *he* is attracted to her because of her bright, vibrant, talkative personality, and *she* is attracted to him because he is strong, solid, and relatively silent and enjoys listening to her going on and on and on. But over the long haul he will need to learn how to communicate well if the pair is to survive together, and she will learn to calm down a bit, learn ways to encourage his talking, and learn how to listen better to others rather than chattering all the time. What initially attracts us to a person may later simply become a huge pain in the neck.

Bernard Murstein created a *stimulus-value-role* (SVR) theory to describe how the birds of a feather flock together idea works in actual practice. He argues that there are three components to this process. First, there is the *stimulus*. Individuals are initially attracted by another person's physical appearance or personality or both. This creates a kind of magnetism that encourages each person to want to get to know more about the other.

They become energized beyond the bounds of friendship. As one woman described it, "There's a bit of magic in the air."

The second component becomes evident as the two get to know each other better and the *value complementarity* process begins. Are they compatible in basic beliefs and values? In this process they begin comparing how they look at the world, often quite cautiously because they are afraid the negotiations might break down. Do their moral views fit together? Job and career goals? Their hopes and dreams? Political philosophies, religious views, on and on, all the different beliefs and values that are important to each individual are likely to surface in one way or another.

The original stimulus that brought them together—physical attractiveness, personality traits, and so forth—cannot keep them together for long, because a stable long-term couple relationship needs agreement on basic ways of thinking about life and the direction they want to go through life together. Relationships based on initial attractiveness alone tend to fail the test of time. If the individuals are relatively satisfied with the results of these discussions and observations, they also begin looking at *role complementarity*, the extent to which they can come together and establish a cooperative working relationship. Who will do what? Who will be the boss? Will there be a boss? Will we share tasks? Will each do separate tasks? Think of the relationship as a dance: role complementarity basically is a process in which the individuals test how well they can dance together.

If these initial processes prove successful, feelings of love are likely to grow between the two. Ira Reiss developed a *Wheel Theory of Love* to explain how a love relationship begins and how it can grow over time. Imagine a wheel that can move back and forth. The development of a loving relationship begins as a couple builds a sense of *rapport* with each other. They find things that are attractive in each other and a feeling of connection, a bond begins to grow. As the two feel more and more comfortable with each other, *self-revelation* begins. They feel safe and so they open up their hearts, a little bit at a time, as they test the water to see if it is truly safe to reveal who they are without fear of being rejected or put down. If all goes well, the wheel continues to turn in a positive direction for the relationship, but if it doesn't go well, the wheel can turn in the negative direction.

But the way the wheel needs to be turning is steadily in a positive direction. A feeling of connection or rapport leads to self-revelation, and self-revelation leads to feelings of *mutual dependency* in which each person wants and needs the other. The fourth stage is called *intimacy need fulfillment,* and it involves the satisfaction a person receives from having personal needs fulfilled. When this happens, a sense of greater intimacy or emotional closeness builds. Love is born.

Rapport ➜ *self-revelation* ➜ *mutual dependency* ➜ *intimacy need fulfillment.*

It can look like this if all is going well, but remember, the wheel can turn forward and backward, and it can stop turning altogether. Developing feelings of love for each other is a delicate process and dependent on many factors: our family background, our religious and spiritual values, our education, and so forth. For example, if a person has been abused as a child and has low self-esteem, the individual may find it difficult to trust other people and so building rapport and opening up oneself to another—self-revelation—may be very difficult. If this is the case, a person may find counseling helpful in her efforts to become more comfortable with herself and others.

No Matter How Similar We Are, We're Still Very Different

In the beginning phases of a relationship, if the individuals are interested in each other—if there's a bit of emotional magic in the air fired by sex hormones and pheromones—it's easy to minimize differences and accentuate similarities. If both individuals want the relationship to succeed, areas of potential conflict can be readily glossed over:

"It's no big deal that she's not a Democrat [or Republican], Catholic [or Protestant], country girl [city woman], hunter [book reader], talker [listener], happy-go-lucky person [serious individual] . . . ."

Whatever the differences, and there are many possibilities, the differences can be smoothed over for a while as we tell ourselves that we're "basically the same in all the important categories." Especially in the early phases of the relationship where romance is in the air, good judgment can fly out the window.

As the relationship progresses, however, the initial excitement steadily begins to cool, and it's harder to keep differences under wrap. Things that might have seemed interesting, quaint, funny or inconsequential rise up and begin to cause concern. For this reason, it's good to spend a significant amount of time together over a relatively lengthy period of time so that the prospective mate can be seen in many different situations and from many different angles.

Entering into a long-term intimate relationship is easily among the most important decisions we will make in our lives—arguably the most important decision of all—and who we choose as a partner should be a genuine choice rather than a potential accident we stumble into, blindly. Some today argue that we choose cars with more care and intelligence than the way we choose partners, and this just might be true in many cases.

Over time the differences will come out, because every human being is unique and different from every other human being. There are bound to be differences. These should not be ignored. The issue then becomes whether or not the differences are important differences that cannot be dealt with successfully or differences that can be managed, negotiated, or seen as differences that strengthen the relationship rather than endanger it.

The story of Jason and Beth illustrates a difference between the two that Beth has chosen over the years to simply adjust to. Both Beth and Jason realize he isn't a great communicator. Beth sometimes wishes that he could be more expressive and communicate his affection for her with more warmth and caring. However, after many years of marriage, she has come to realize that he does do things to express his love and concern for her. They may be things like helping with housework or taking care of her car, but they are his way of sharing their lives together and showing that he cares. Beth can learn to live with Jason's difficulty in expressing affection, and, likewise, Jason can learn to become a little bit better at expressing affection, step-by-step. This illustrates a good solution in which both move somewhat toward a middle ground that both are comfortable with.

"I Wish We Wouldn't Have Wasted so Many Years Trying to Fix Each Other"

An older woman was talking about her love for her husband who had died recently. She talked about their life together, through 44 years of thick and thin. How they met, how they fell in love, early marriage, raising four children together, the inevitable crises they faced together, the agony of his sudden, unexpected death.

She talked about how they both grew up on the farm, both were Lutherans, both were middle-class and middle-American in heritage. And how there were some annoying personality traits that each had, causing exasperation and hard feelings between the two on occasion.

As many couples do, from early on in the marriage they both set out in subtle and not-so-subtle ways to try to change the other person so that the differences would magically disappear and they would suddenly become totally alike, totally in synch, the perfect match.

It didn't work. Her efforts to change him usually backfired. He would take offense and fire back about her shortcomings. Likewise, his efforts to change her inevitably went for nothing. "I am who I am," she would say, and from her perspective that meant that the argument was over (or certainly should be over).

The widow grew silent and looked very thoughtful. Her expression reflected the pain she was feeling: "I wish," she said, "that we wouldn't have wasted so many years trying to fix each other."

The fact of the matter is, most couples probably spend too much time trying to *fix* each other. Through time, it is probably the case that most people do start to converge somewhere toward the middle, in terms of personality, beliefs, values, behaviors, and so forth. The act of living together for a long period of time forces tiny adjustments in each individual, smoothing the relationship and making day-by-day life more pleasant and workable. But, the quest to totally revamp the other person's personality and behavior is likely to be doomed from the beginning.

Broadly speaking, marital relationships fail for two major reasons: 1) people make the wrong choice in the beginning; or 2) the relationship cannot withstand the test of time and the stresses, strains and temptations that life inevitably brings. For many couples, the relationship fails because the two major reasons combine to cause trouble.

The first thing we can do, then, to set out on the right foot is to make a good choice. One useful way to do this is to make an inventory of your strengths as a couple. What are the strengths of your relationship? What are the areas of potential growth in your relationship? In the next chapter, we will assess how well you're doing together.

Look for the Good Things in Your Partner And You Will Find Them

In the final analysis, it is important to remember that a focus on strengths tends to make life go smoother and happier. If we insist on digging up dirt on our partner, we're going to find it. Look for problems and you will find them, because no human being is perfect (and if a person were, that person would be impossible to live with!).

Similarly, if we look for the strengths and positive aspects of our partner, we're likely to see many things that merit our attention and praise.

Is this a way of looking at life through rose-colored glasses? Are we saying that you should ignore problems altogether? Not at all. What we are saying is that it's easy to focus on the negative, and when this happens we easily can forget all the positive things that brought us together as a couple in the first place. If a child gets an 87% or a 92% on an exam, doesn't it make sense to spend some time focusing on the fact that he did so well? Does it make sense to jump right in and pound him for the 13% or 8% that wasn't right? The search for perfection can be oppressive for everyone involved.

Likewise, spend time praising and thanking your partner for all the good things he or she does to make your life joyful. When we do this, it is likely that your partner will continue to do these nice things. Since couple relationships work both ways, concentrate on ways to make your partner's life more joyful, more fulfilling. Relationships work better when we both know how to scratch each other's back, in a manner of speaking. *Accentuate the positive* is old advice that works extraordinarily well most of the time. Some examples of how this works:

> That was really neat of you to fill the tank of my car up with gas. I was in a hurry this morning and it made me happy to see I didn't have to run to the service station.

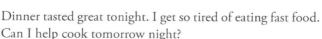

> Dinner tasted great tonight. I get so tired of eating fast food. Can I help cook tomorrow night?

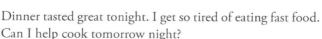

41

That was kind of you to call my Mom and talk with her. She gets so lonely without Dad around now, and she enjoys hearing a man's voice.

Very Short Stories from Real People

Gregg and I both vote in every election. Usually we cancel each other out as he is a Republican and I am a Democrat. We just never agree so we agree to disagree on the major candidates.

I know a young couple who married and divorced within a year. They didn't go together very long before they got married and she never saw her husband ever drink. After the wedding he took up his old habits in front of her and felt he was finally done with the perfect behavior he practiced while actively courting her. She felt he made her life miserable with his drinking and soon divorced him.

My husband leaves little sticky notes around the house with a smiley face or a heart to remind me that he loves me when he is going out of town. If I have been out of town, I come home and find a sticky note heart right at my eye level by the coat closet. It makes me smile and feel like I am appreciated and loved.

We decided that we would not allow our parents to talk negatively about our partners. We say, "I know that you have some feelings about _____ that I don't agree with, and I would rather you not say them to me."

When my daughter calls to tell me about her in-laws, I say, "Have you and _____ discussed how you feel about this?" When she says, "No," I say, "Talk to him about it and help him understand how their comments or their behaviors make you feel." Suggest that he use the words in the above illustration with his parents!

Discussion Questions

1. What are the strengths of each of your families of origin? What are the areas of potential growth from each of your perspectives?
2. Prioritize which ones you will focus on in your couple relationship and work together to make the extended family relationship better.
3. Make a family tree of your family of origin. What are the similarities? What are the differences? Combine the two trees into your new couple family tree.
4. How does your family of origin celebrate important events?
5. Discuss current events. How are each of your views similar? How are they different? How do you deal with these differences as a couple? Are there areas where you could improve how you deal with your differences?

Tips for Strengthening Your Relationship

1. What are the strengths of each of your families of origin? What are the weaknesses from each of your perspectives? Prioritize which ones you will focus on in your couple relationship, and work together to help make extended family relationships better.
2. Take time to be in love each day. What are the things that remind you that you are in love? Holding hands, sitting beside each other to talk about your day, taking a walk around the neighborhood together, and so forth.
3. Pray together at meals or sit together and meditate about the meaningful things in your life.
4. Make up a note that says *10 Things I Love About You* and post it somewhere to surprise your partner.

CHAPTER 4

What Are Our Strengths as a Couple?
How Can We Build on Them?

Assessing Your Strengths

It always amazes us to see this, but in our experience we find that couples often do not have a clear picture of the strengths of their relationship. Why is this the case? We live in a problem-oriented society: The focus is almost always on defining problems and finding solutions. Thus, couples often have a very clear picture of what's wrong with their relationship, but have not spent any time whatsoever at focusing on their strengths.

The trouble with this approach is that we use our strengths to deal with our problems. And if we don't have an understanding of our strengths, it is difficult to see how problems can be dealt with successfully.

Our focus here will be on the strengths of your relationship with your partner and how these strengths can be built upon to develop an even stronger bond with each other. A useful way to begin the discussion of couple strengths is to fill out the *American Couple Strengths Inventory*.

As educators we have used inventories such as this with couples for many years and have found that many couples are delighted to learn about their strengths. It is quite common for a spouse to say, "I always think about our problems and this is the first time I've really thought about our strengths. It's really neat to see how many good things we have in our marriage."

Taking the *American Couple Strengths Inventory*

The *American Couple Strengths Inventory* has evolved from research that Nick Stinnett began in 1974. More than 27,000 family members have participated in this research in the U.S. and 38 other countries around the world. These questions for couples have been tested and validated in America and similar inventories have been developed in other countries for use in very different cultures. What is remarkable to us is that couple strengths and family strengths from culture to culture are remarkably similar; much more similar than different.

On the basis of research over several decades we believe that a useful model for describing couple and family strengths includes six major strengths: appreciation and affection for each other; commitment to the couple and the family; positive communication; enjoyable time together; a sense of spiritual well-being and shared values; and the ability to manage stress and crisis effectively. These strengths or *positive relationship qualities* are all interrelated with each other and really cannot be broken apart: appreciation and affection are related to positive communication, a sense of spiritual well-being and shared values enhance a couple's ability to manage stress and crisis effectively, and so forth. Each quality builds on the others, and if a couple has one quality they are quite likely to have many others. The key is that if you look for strengths in your relationship, you will find them, and if you nurture these strengths, they will grow.

So, begin this fascinating process by filling out the couple strengths inventory together.

American Couple Strengths Inventory

Take your time filling this inventory out together. Discuss your response to each item with each other. Remember: No one is right and no one is wrong. These are your honest perceptions and you can practice positive communication by discussing your answers: why you are in agreement on some items and why you have different answers on other items.

If you really find the activity enjoyable, you might want to fill the *ACSI* out over several days: perhaps filling out and discussing one or two strengths each time you sit down together. Find a quiet place to do this so you can concentrate on each other and how you feel.

On the next pages, rate each quality in your relationship using three possible choices: an *S* for a *strength*; a *G* for an *area of potential growth* (something you would like to see improved in your relationship); and a *NA* for *not applicable in our relationship.*

Remember: No couple on earth has a perfect relationship. You will find that you have some strengths and you will find that you have some areas of potential growth. The aim is to find your strengths and use them to build an even stronger relationship. If you would like to discuss these issues further with a professional, we recommend you set up an appointment with a National Council on Family Relations Certified Family Life Educator or an American Association for Marital and Family Therapy Certified Marital and Family Therapist.

Principle Investigators:

John DeFrain, Ph.D.
Professor and Extension Family
and Community Development Specialist

Department of Child, Youth and Family Studies
University of Nebraska–Lincoln

Linda Skogrand, Ph.D.
Associate Professor and Extension Family Life Specialist
Department of Family, Consumer and Human Development
Utah State University, Logan
Phone: 435-797-8183
Email: lindas@ext.usu.edu

Appreciation And Affection

(S = *Strength*; G = *Area of Potential Growth*; and NA = *Not Applicable in Our Relationship*)

Name	Name	
		caring for each other
		respect for each other
		respect for individuality
		physical and emotional affection
		tolerance
		playfulness
		humor
		put downs and sarcasm are rare
		we are both committed to helping enhance each other's self-esteem
		a feeling of security
		safety
		we genuinely like each other, and we like being with each other
		Overall rating of ***appreciation and affection*** in our relationship

Commitment		
(S = *Strength*; G = *Area of Potential Growth*; and NA = *Not Applicable in Our Relationship*)		
Name	Name	
		trust
		honesty
		dependability
		fidelity or faithfulness
		we are one
		we are family
		sacrifice
		sharing
		Overall rating of **commitment** in our relationship

Positive Communication		
(S = *Strength*; G = *Area of Potential Growth*; and NA = *Not Applicable in Our Relationship*)		
Name	Name	
		open, straightforward communication
		discussion rather than lectures
		positive, not negative, communication
		cooperative, not competitive
		nonblaming
		a few squabbles occur, but generally are consensus building, rather than a winner and a loser
		compromise
		agreeing to disagree on occasion

		acceptance of the notion that differences can be a strength in our marriage and that we do not have to be exactly the same
		Overall rating of **positive communication** in our relationship

		Enjoyable Time Together (S = *Strength*; G = *Area of Potential Growth*; and NA = *Not Applicable in Our Relationship*)
Name	Name	
		good things take time, and we take time to be with each other
		we share quality time, and in great quantity we enjoy each other's company
		serendipitous (unplanned, spontaneous) good times
		simple, inexpensive good times
		Overall rating of the **enjoyable time** we share together

		Spiritual Well-Being And Shared Values (S = *Strength*; G = *Area of Potential Growth*; and NA = *Not Applicable in Our Relationship*)
Name	Name	
		happiness
		optimism
		hope
		a sense of peace
		mental health

		a functional religion or set of shared ethical values, which guide us through life's challenges
		oneness with God
		oneness with Nature
		oneness with that which is sacred to us in life
		supportive extended family members
		involvement in the community, and support from the community
		the world is our home and we feel comfortable in it
		Overall rating of *spiritual well-being* and *shared values*

The Ability To Manage Stress And Crisis Effectively (S = *Strength*; G = *Area of Potential Growth*; and NA = *Not Applicable in Our Relationship*)		
Name	Name	
		share feelings
		understand each other
		help each other
		forgiveness
		"don't worry, be happy"
		growing through crises together
		patience
		resilience (the ability to "hang in there")
		Overall rating of *our ability to manage stress and crisis effectively*

Overall Ratings Of Our Couple Relationship		
(S = *Strength*; G = *Area of Potential Growth*; and NA = *Not Applicable in Our Relationship*)		
Name	Name	
		the level of ***closeness*** with each other
		the level of ***satisfaction*** with each other
		the level of ***happiness*** with each other
		the level of ***strength*** of our relationship

Discussing Your Strengths

It is important to remember that each partner is likely to have a different view of the relationship they have with each other and what is happening in the family. Even though you may eat at the same table and witness the same things happening in your life and the life of your extended family, you are very likely to *see things differently*. Professionals who work with families like to say that, "We don't see the world *the way it is*. We see the world *the way we are*." In other words, each individual filters the world through her or his own lens of perception.

For example, what might seem to be a friendly joke to one person could seem like a very hostile attack to another person. Or, what seems to one person like a kind offer of assistance might feel like an imposition to another individual. Similarly, the question, "How are you doing?" might sound snoopy to one person while another would welcome the opportunity to share thoughts and feelings. Couples are quite likely to interpret what is happening in the relationship and in the family quite differently from each other. This is why it is important to continuously discuss your perceptions of what is going on and to compare your perceptions with your partner. You may be very happy with what is happening and you may find that your partner may be very upset. Only clear and open communication can smooth out your path together.

In discussing the strengths of your relationship, you inevitably found that you have different perceptions. You could decide that this is a problem, or you could instead define these differences as an opportunity

51

for growth: a chance to honestly discuss, in a friendly and loving manner, the fascinating fact that the world looks different to each of you in some interesting ways.

People who love each other don't always agree, and they would be foolish to try to stamp out all disagreement. Rather, it is wise to recognize that *you will automatically have different views* and then enjoy creating new strategies so your different ways of looking at the world mean you can still continue to live happily together.

In regard to your strengths as a couple, discuss your different perceptions and then come to a consensus on the strengths that you can both agree upon, and the areas of potential growth that you also can agree upon.

Building on Your Strengths: A Useful and Fun Activity

Try this simple exercise: pick two of the couple strengths that you agree upon and write brief plans (in the space provided) that you can follow for a month to make these fine qualities that you have even better:

Our Strength: #1

Our Plan for Enhancing Strength #1:

Our Strength: #2

Our Plan for Enhancing Strength #2:

Now choose an area of potential growth—an area in your couple relationship that is not yet a strength but that you would like to work together on to develop into a couple strength. In the space provided, write down the area of potential growth you will work on together, and your plan for doing this.

An Area of Potential Growth We Would Like to Improve in Our Relationship:

Our Plan for Improving This Area of Potential Growth:

For a month, work together on enhancing the two strengths you have chosen to focus on; and, work together on improving the area of potential growth you have chosen. Mark your calendar for a month from today. Make a note that you will have a date together to sit down in a relaxed, loving and friendly manner and talk about your progress in building on your strengths as a couple!

Very Short Stories from Real People

Several years ago I gave my husband a small note paper with Ten Things I Love About You written at the top and the list of what I saw as his top 10 personal strengths. The list is still in a prominent place on his desk. It is a little rumpled and faded now. He says it reminds him every day of his reflection in my mirror of love and he tries to be that person.

My husband and I are both teachers. We are both good listeners and we communicate well with our students. However, at home, we tend to forget to use those skills with each other because we are tired, over-committed, and less than tolerant. We have chosen to give each other a cue by saying, "Honey, can you say that to me another way?" This reminds us to take a breath, focus on our loved one and show our appreciation for them by giving them the same courtesy we give our students.

My husband and I are both teachers. We are both good listeners and we communicate well with our students. However, at home, we tend to forget to use those skills with each other because we are tired, over-committed, and less than tolerant. We have chosen to give each other a cue by saying, "Honey, can you say that to me another way?" This reminds us to take a breath, focus on our loved one and show our appreciation for them by giving them the same courtesy we give our students.

One of us has the strength of planning. Actually, over-planning! And, one of us has the strength of finding joy and connections to bigger things if we just let things develop. Since these are two opposite strengths, we rely on each other for balance. I let him plan the structure of the event and then I add the fun and push the edges for flexibility. If I do this in love with good communication and praise for his strengths, and he breathes deeply with appreciation for my strengths, we can usually find that balance and have a great time. If I push the boundaries of flexibility or he pushes the rigidity of the plan, we can ruin a perfectly great time together. So, over time, we have made this a goal: Seek balance in all things with love and understanding.

My husband had always been a member of a church. Even when he was a small boy and his parents were divorced, he went to church with a neighbor friend. Attending church, serving on boards and giving money for missions are all good things. Until we married and began to work on our faith together, my husband had never felt spirituality. Now, many years later, we have a week-long vacation in the mountains in the summer and hike and just enjoy nature. For us, this strengthens our faith to do the work in our church. Spirituality is not confined to denomination or a building. It is in everything we see, everything we say, everything we touch. The couple grows so much closer once it discovers its couple spirituality.

Don and Donna moved around from state to state. They changed jobs and houses and furniture and friends. One of them wanted to live in the desert and one wanted to live in the mountains. They would tolerate each other's desire for physical location for so long and then that was it! It was time to move. As they aged, they began to see that this transitional life style was physically harder to accomplish. They wonder now what life would have been like if they had lived in one place and rented or purchased a place in the other location for frequent trips during the year. Their goal now is to make a plan together for the rest of their life using the information they gathered about each other's strengths from the *American Couple Strengths Inventory*.

Discussion Questions

1. What personal strengths attracted you to each other?
2. How do you celebrate each other's strengths? Example: Words of affirmation.
3. How can your strengths become your weaknesses and how will you recognize the change?
4. How will you each solve the issue of differing perceptions of a comment or a situation?
5. What will be the outcome of regularly filling out your *Couple Strengths Inventory*?

Tips for Strengthening Your Relationship

1. To affirm your partner's strengths, make a list *Ten Things I Like About You* and post in a prominent location.
2. Plan a date night once a month to celebrate each other's strengths and the strengths you create as a couple.
3. Compare your progress on couple strengths and set a new measurable goal. Example: We will stop any communication that sounds like blame and restate the message in a positive, loving way.
4. Just as you try to *catch kids in positive behaviors*, catch your spouse in strengths behavior and reward him/her with praise.
5. Thank your Creator as a couple for bringing your strengths together.

CHAPTER 5

Positive Communication
And the Development of Emotional
Intimacy

Men and Women Are Likely
To Communicate Differently

A great deal has been written in recent years on the notion that men and women are likely to communicate differently from each other. Men, as the argument goes, are likely to be strong and silent. Men, it is said, are less communicative because their childhood experiences were very different from those of little girls: While little girls were talking and laughing and bickering over their dolls and tea sets, little boys were outside happily bashing each other on the playing field.

Women, it is said, are socialized as little girls by their mothers and girlfriends. They are socialized to be especially communicative, keenly aware of the thoughts and feelings of others. Since women, on average, are smaller and less physically powerful than men, girls from a very young age develop their verbal skills to compensate for their lack of muscle when push comes to shove in a conflict with boys and men. As the analogy goes, girls are like mice in the middle of the living room, and boys are like elephants. The mouse always needs to know where the elephant is to avoid getting trampled, but the elephant doesn't have to think about much at all.

The trouble with generalizations such as these is that they do work sometimes, but many other times they don't work at all. One woman, thinking about her strong and silent husband, told her female friend quite emphatically that, "If you want someone to talk to, marry a woman!" This just might be very true in this particular woman's life, but many other women find sensitive, thoughtful and talkative husbands who are very capable of communicating positively. And, in some marriages there are reversals from the stereotypic partnership: Instead of a strong and silent husband and a friendly and communicative wife, the roles are reversed and he is the talker while she is the quiet one.

Fortunately, the truth of the matter is that every partnership is different and generalizations do not work very well. The beauty of this situation is that couples are forced, from the very beginning, not to think in stereotypes and jump to easy conclusions about each other. They have to learn how to communicate well: listen with empathy and talk clearly, honestly, and openly.

Individuals from Different Cultures Sometimes Communicate Differently

As we noted earlier, socialization of children in early childhood can be quite different for boys and girls. This leads to the development of what could be called *boy culture* and *girl culture*, and confusion often does occur when the two cultures come in contact with each other and misunderstandings happen. Talking about boys and girls this way, as we have said, can be overblown but is useful to keep in the back of one's mind when trying to understand the ups and downs of male and female relationships. To paraphrase what cultural anthropologists commonly believe, the greatest distance between two people is not measured in space but culture. How we grew up, and the world as it exists today, makes a tremendous difference in how we view the world.

Similarly, there are countless other cultural differences besides boy culture and girl culture that can cause difficulty in partnerships. Though people tend to marry others who are relatively similar in terms of culture—similar in education, ethnicity, social class, religion and spiritual values, and so forth—most relationships pair people who do bring somewhat different cultural backgrounds to the partnership. *He* might be from the country, *she* from the city. He might be Jewish, she Muslim. He might be African American, she might be Lakota. The possibilities are infinite.

Likewise, as you will remember, individuals bring elements of the cultures of their families of origin into the marital partnership. These family cultures brought to the marriage from our childhood backgrounds can be very different. Finally, individual differences can be quite dramatic. Her personality is likely to have elements that are quite different from his personality. These differences might not have anything to do with maleness or femaleness, but may be a reflection of the unique aspects of each individual's personality. No two human beings are completely alike. We are all, just as snowflakes, unique.

The best way to deal with these differences is not to treat them as problems but as fascinating opportunities. As one husband noted, "I'm delighted she is different from me in many ways. I always have to be on my toes because she looks at the world differently, and our different views strengthen us as a couple. Two different heads really are better than one."

Communication Is a Cooperative Effort

For communication to work really well, it needs to be a cooperative effort and not a competitive effort. The goal of communication for couples is a stronger, happier and more loving relationship. This goal is not reached by engaging in verbal battles with the aim of winning the argument over one's partner. Competitive communication can be called a *zero-sum game*. My win and your loss sum to zero: 1-1 = 0. My "thrill of victory" plus your "agony of defeat" add up to nothing.

Cooperative communication, on the other hand, is a win-win process: 1 + 1 = 2. We are not opposing forces trying to overcome an adversary or take something away from our adversary. Rather, we are on the same team: we work together as a team cooperatively, and we find a solution to the problems we face *together*. In the heat of discussion, of course, this can be difficult to do. So, when the discussion starts to boil over, it is important to withdraw from battle for a few hours or a few minutes until each individual has calmed down and is ready to be on the same team again. Sometimes our emotions get the better of us and we say and do things that we will regret later. In a discussion if we see this coming, it is important to back off until we can calm down and be loving toward each other again.

Strong families and happy couples do not treat differences of opinion as if they were reasons to go to war. Such an approach is counterproductive and hurtful to everyone involved.

Building a Relationship Versus Telling Someone What to Do

Happy couples are very respectful toward each other. One important element of respect is demonstrating that you are equals in the relationship. Each individual's opinion is valued, both individuals are of equal importance, both have equal power in the relationship, both have one vote in the democracy that is the marriage.

When the relationship is approached this way, it is likely to thrive. The partners are in a position to genuinely care for each other. If, on the other hand, the goal is not to build a strong and loving relationship but, instead, to have a partnership in which one person is the boss and the other the follower, genuine love for each other is difficult to develop. Think about the situation this way: If your boss at work is genuinely bossy, you are not prone to like the person. And, you certainly are not likely to *love* the person. We might "respect" or fear our boss, but if a boss acts in a condescending, pushy and bullish manner, good feelings toward this person are likely to diminish.

Some marriages, unfortunately, operate this way, and when an individual forgets that it is more important to build a strong and caring relationship than it is to tell one's partner what to do all the time, it can spell disaster for the long-term survival of the marriage.

Nonverbal Communication and Self-Disclosure

A great deal of what we say to each other is said without words: Our body language gives messages to our partner that may not fit with the words of love we profess for each other. We may say we feel connected to our partner but our face or body will convey boredom, irritation, inattention, stress or the sense that we are overwhelmed by life.

"How are you doing?" one might ask.

"Fine," the partner might reply, when her body clearly shows that she is feeling miserable.

In a loving relationship it is important to pay close attention to not only what people say but how they are really *feeling*. When partners communicate on a genuine feeling level, they understand each other well and are likely to feel empathy, concern and love for each other.

This is difficult to do because we learn very quickly as young children how to hide our feelings out of fear of being teased, picked on, put down. We learn very early how to defend ourselves from other human beings bent on giving us grief for grief's sake by simply hiding our feelings and, when push comes to shove, fighting back.

Couples often take this foolish behavior that they learned on the playground as young children into marriage, and it simply doesn't work.

Taking a defensive position in an intimate relationship is a recipe for disaster. When we try to hide from our partner who we really are, our body language and the nonverbal cues that we exhibit convey the real message that we are trying to cover up.

If our partner senses our true feelings and takes this as an opportunity to attack us, the battle is on. If, on the other hand, our partner has a well-developed sense of empathy—can see the world through our eyes and experience some of the feelings we feel—then the chance for a genuinely loving relationship grows and is nurtured by the caring and compassion we have shown.

When we come home from a long day at work or school or out in the community, it is common to ask each other: "What did you do today?" This is a reasonable way to begin a conversation with our partner or our children. But if we want genuine communication and understanding of each other, there is a more important follow-up question: "How do you feel about your day?" This focuses on how the day really went from an emotional standpoint and whether we like it or not, our lives are full of emotions that need to be recognized and honored.

If the day has worn us down, we need to acknowledge this to ourselves and to our partners. We need to talk about the ups and downs of our lives, disclose to each other who we *really* are, and build a relationship on honesty and trust. This is called self-disclosure, the process of letting our partner know what is really happening in our life and how it feels to us from the inside.

The key is to find a partner who is not afraid of self-disclosure, who sees the importance of letting others into his real world, and who honors and respects and appreciates the true feelings that others express. When we become more transparent about our lives and our feelings, other people are likely to be more transparent or open about themselves, and we soon learn that we are not all that different from each other: we can be happy, we can be sad, we can be angry, we can be bored, we can be engaged and connected to each other, we can feel disengaged and isolated. We're all only human and humans share a common set of emotions that everyone feels at one time or another. When we are successful in self-disclosing genuine beliefs and feelings with each other, both partners are likely to feel supported and secure in the relationship.

Countless great marriages exist, proving that it is possible to create an open and honest relationship, while many marriages fail because the partners have not learned how to genuinely communicate with each other. Altogether this demonstrates that communication is worth the effort, though the task will not be easy and it is an ongoing task that lasts a lifetime together for a couple.

Listening: Why We Have Two Ears and One Mouth

Listening, really listening to each other with not only our heads but our hearts, is the key to positive communication.

Many people make the mistake of thinking that talking is the key to communication and so "they fill the sky with words." In reality, sound relationships are built because both partners are good at listening to each other. This is done effectively by asking good questions and, even more important, asking good follow-up questions:

"How are you doing?"

"How do you feel about that?"

"What are you going to do in response?"

"Where can you find some answers?"

"Are there people who understand what you're going through and can help?"

A genuinely open conversation means that both people are talking precisely and honestly, focusing on not only facts but feelings, and focusing so that they can really hear and feel what the other person is trying to convey. When we listen to another person closely and with interest, we are paying them a great compliment: We are saying, "I care about you, I respect you, I want to understand you better and learn how you see the world, I want to get close to you."

People who are poor listeners are not really listening at all. They are simply waiting for the person who is talking to be quiet so that they can have the stage again. Poor listeners are not really hearing what is being said; instead, they are simply using the time to practice in their mind what they are going to say next. Poor listeners are generally not attractive people to others, and are not likely to be very satisfying as partners.

As the old saying goes, we were born with two ears and only one mouth. Therefore, we should work twice as hard to listen rather than just talk. We might have even happier marriages if we had been born with 10 ears and one mouth.

Aggressive Communication And Assertive Communication

When we are trying to win an argument, we are likely to become aggressive in our communication style. Aggressive communication aims to put down, control or hurt the other person. Aggressors foolishly believe that by attacking the other person their own personal self-esteem will be built up; by hurting someone else they will somehow manage to feel better about themselves. Aggressive communication simply does not work in an intimate, loving relationship. It always causes much more harm than good, and a great deal of careful effort must be invested in rebuilding the relationship after an aggressive outburst has occurred. Aggressive communication drives people apart rather than bringing them together.

Assertive communication, on the other hand, focuses on expressing who you are and how you feel without attacking the other person. Assertive communication grants us the right to be who we are and feel what we feel without infringing on the rights of the other person or putting her down. The goal of assertive communication is not to win the argument; the goal of assertive communication is to find a way to live happily together while, at the same time, honoring the individual rights of our partner.

Aggressive communicators assume that life is a battle and they need to be prepared to fight and fight hard to win over their opponents, even if the opponent might be their partner or their children. Assertive communicators assume that life is a gift and we all need to find ways to cherish each other and help each other grow in ways that meet our individual needs while preserving the loving relationship we have with each other.

Why Avoidance Doesn't Work

When one partner relies on an aggressive communication style, it sometimes seems easier or safer to the partner to avoid conflict and cover up genuine feelings. This avoidance style of communication might have short-term benefits—conflicts may be avoided and glossed over for a while—but eventually the long-term consequences are likely to occur. When one partner, over time, is aggressive and the other partner hides true feelings and who she/he really is and constantly gives in to the other, the one avoiding conflict is likely to disengage from the relationship emotionally. A disengaged marriage is a marriage that is failing and likely to end in divorce.

A Word on Positive Self-Talk

Before we end our discussion here on positive communication, it is important to say a few words about the importance of positive self-talk. Everyone talks to themselves—sometimes out loud and sometimes only in their minds—and these conversations we have with ourselves can be positive, self-esteem building conversations or they can be times when we beat ourselves down.

Rather than wasting energy belittling ourselves, it is important to focus on the positive, emphasizing our strengths, and planning how we will use these strengths to work out difficulties we are facing in life. We need to focus on the gifts we have and how we put these gifts to use.

In sum, we all need to learn to talk with ourselves with the same amount of love and respect that we talk with our best friends.

What, Then, Have We Seen Here About Positive Communication and the Development Of Emotional Intimacy?

As children and young people we learn quickly about the warm encounters and the bruising encounters we experience in life that are called human relationships. We learn the joy of kind, thoughtful and loving relationships and we learn about the emotional pain one experiences when a relationship fails. There are many barriers to positive relationships and emotional intimacy: cultural differences between boys and girls, men and women; cultural differences between people of different ages and from different ethnic groups, social classes, educational backgrounds, and with different religious/spiritual beliefs.

However, learning the art and science of positive communication can bridge these differences and make sound intimate relationships likely. Keys to open, honest and straightforward communication include the fact that we need to see communication as a cooperative effort rather than a competition between each other; that building an intimate and loving relationship is not about telling other people what to do, but instead focusing on the process of creating a bond with each other; that nonverbal communication sometimes sends important messages that we may not know we are sending, and that self-disclosure is essential if we are to communicate well with each other; that learning to talk clearly and calmly is important, but learning to listen with one's heart is absolutely essential; that aggression doesn't work in an intimate relationship, nor does avoiding issues; and that an assertive communication style for both partners ensures that each feels free to express personal feelings and beliefs while respecting and honoring the feelings and beliefs of her partner.

As the adage goes:

People forget what you say
They forget what you do
But they don't forget
How you make them feel.

Very Short Stories from Real People

> I fell in love with her because she was so wonderfully different from me. But after we were married, I would get upset with her because she was so different from me. And then, finally, it hit me: The differences are what made me love her in the first place, so relax and enjoy them!

> I was traveling the other day and enjoyed listening about a dozen times to a country song, "Waiting on a Woman." The song reminded me of the caring attitude my Dad has had all these years about not hurrying Mom to get done or be ready. He took her for what she was, and enjoyed her that way.

65

It's amazing to me that in my family, two siblings growing up in the same household had very different childhood experiences with one being physically abused and the other not. As a result, their adult perspectives continue to be very different.

Promises made at marriage can sometimes lead to communication problems. I remember my grandparents living separate lives in different parts of the same house for months on end while they were at odds over religious differences.

My girlfriend and I have a special relationship but we have huge struggles with communication. She is emotionally vulnerable and keeps all her thoughts and feelings inside. I don't know how to break through that barrier, especially since she has shared so little about her past.

Discussion Questions

1. Think about the family you grew up in. How did your parents communicate over the years? What other couples have you watched communicate? Give some examples from growing up where you were taught how to communicate.
2. As the saying goes, "Children should be seen and not heard." What does this teach about communication? Are there other examples?
3. How can a couple change *competitive communication* (1-1=0) into *cooperative communication* (1+1=2)?
4. Why is it important to be a good listener? How can we all become better listeners?

5. Describe some barriers to communication that you have personally observed.

Tips for Strengthening Your Relationship

1. Learn to trust each other by using self-disclosure techniques. Each partner needs to open up and be more honest and transparent.
2. Focus on building a bond between the two of you. Find little things you love to share. Be sure to follow up on your ideas.
3. Anything mentionable is manageable: If you can talk about it, you can figure out a way to prevent it from becoming a barrier in your relationship.
4. When you're talking, you don't learn anything because you already know what you're going to say. When you're listening, you learn *a lot*. Listen carefully first, then figure out what you are going to say. Don't think about your response while your partner is talking, because you won't really be hearing what he or she is saying.
5. We see the world not the way *it is*, but the way *we are*. Our experiences develop our perspective, which influences our communication.
6. Couples who want to build cooperative communication face problems together as a team, rather than competing with each other. Find ways to work together more.
7. Before tempers flair, make a plan together that allows either of you to leave the room without explanation. Take a break for as long as is needed to cool down—hopefully not very long—and resume the conversation as soon as you are able. Don't try to avoid working together to solve the problem, and don't have a temper tantrum. These approaches just don't work at all.
8. Don't play games when communicating with loved ones. Loving relationships are too important for that!

CHAPTER 6

Differences Are Inevitable: How to Resolve Conflicts

Conflict and Anger

It is very clear that differences between couples are inevitable. We are all unique individuals, we come from unique families, and we have unique community and cultural influences that have affected our development as human beings. When we pair up as couples these inevitable differences do not simply go away. Instead, they are likely to become magnified over time and sometimes turn into a source of frustration between the partners:

If he loves me so much, why would he say such stupid things?
If she really understood me, she would not even think about doing that!

Much of our frustration with our partner hinges on the silly belief we all harbor that, "If he loves me he should understand. He should be able to read my mind. I shouldn't have to tell him what I need. He should know!"

The fact of the matter is, however, that love does not conquer all. Feelings of love for each other are very powerful. There is no doubt about that. But just because we have these feelings does not guarantee that we are going to understand each other and always say and do the perfect thing.

Instead, our love for each other should serve as motivation for each of us to learn how to communicate effectively with each other and find out how to resolve our inevitable differences and the conflicts that grow out of these differences.

Differences lead to conflicting ways of looking at the world and our life together as partners, and these conflicts often generate anger. The solution to this problem that all couples face is learning to have the courage to communicate well with each other: listening with our hearts, speaking in a loving way with each other, and creating a future together that warms our heart and gives us a feeling of security.

None of this is easy. Always trying to look for the good in each other can be difficult, especially when we feel stressed and under-appreciated.

Conflict and Love

Can you love a person and still get mad at them?

Of course. Everyone gets mad at their loved ones. But the key is not to go off the deep end and say or do things that are damaging and hurtful.

In fact, we can do the wrong thing from two different directions: We can get so angry with our partner that we become emotionally abusive or physically abusive. This is a terrible mistake and leads to the destruction of the relationship and could be the death of love. In a happy and healthy relationship, there is no place for any kind of abuse.

From the other direction, we can try to avoid being angry at our partner so much that it leads to emotional disengagement. In this scenario, we work so hard to cover up our feelings, to plaster a fake smile on our face, and we do this for so long that we have nothing left but the fake smile. The love underneath has dried up and blown away, leaving what marital and family therapists call a *devitalized relationship*. This type of relationship is devoid of all life, empty of all energy, lacking all feeling for our partner, without love. Devitalized relationships are more common among married people than hostile and angry relationships, and are especially common among those couples seeking a divorce.

So, if we can destroy the partnership by being too angry and abusive, and also by being too avoidant of conflict, what is the solution? How do we strike the right balance?

1. Recognize that differences are normal and inevitable. That all loving relationships have differences.
2. Recognize that differences can lead to conflict.
3. Recognize that conflict can lead to anger, abuse or avoidance.

4. Recognize that successful relationships always have a little give and take: Each person has to give in on occasion if the partnership is to work. Compromise is an essential tool.
5. Learn to deal with anger in a peaceful, loving and caring way. Avoid getting too worked up emotionally. Focus on the facts and how to solve the problem together. Again, is this easy? Of course not. Is the effort to learn how to deal with life's inevitable conflicts in a peaceful way worth it? Absolutely.

And, are couples capable of being perfect in their efforts to build a loving relationship? No. But they do have the ability to try hard to build a more loving relationship than they have today. Improvement is always possible.

The Truth About Anger

Let's spend some more time here looking at couples and anger. Here are some things partners say regarding their anger that are worth thinking about and discussing:

- **"He enjoys getting mad."** For many partners, this is true. Being angry can be fun. They feel powerful when they are angry, and self-righteous. Their feelings of anger in some sort of twisted logic make them feel as if they are right and righteous, when really they are only angry. They feel as if they are winning an argument when their partner cringes or hides or runs away in fear. They feel in control. They feel special. But, this kind of behavior is nothing more than *emotional abuse* and has no place in a loving relationship. In addition, these feelings of anger can give a person an almost sexual high, and couples who have violent verbal and physical conflicts often resolve the situation soon after a big blow-up argument with sex. This, of course, is a mistake, because it gets love and anger all mixed together, and anger is not an expression of love. It's just an expression of anger.
- **"She made me mad. It's her fault!"** The truth is, no one *makes* us angry. We *let ourselves become angry* as a response to others' behavior. There are better ways in which we could choose to respond besides anger: We could take a brief emotional time-out

until we calm down and then come back to the discussion with our partner when we both can be rational and not explosive.

- **"She made me mad. That's why I hit her!"** Again, our partners do not make us angry. Our partners do not make us react violently toward them. We can choose how to respond to our partners. If we are interested in creating a loving and caring partnership, violence has no place.

- **"She's not an angry person. The alcohol made her angry."** This is a common belief that can be deadly. Somehow the drinker is not responsible for her or his behavior. The fact of the matter is, however, that no one else *made the individual drink* and, therefore, no one should be abused emotionally or physically because of another person's drinking. Going along with a drinker's excuses for bad behavior is a big mistake.

- **"I had to yell at her. If I didn't, I might have exploded."** Some partners rationalize their anger by saying that it is better than the explosive violence that would inevitably follow. This is nonsense. Angry words tend to lead to violent behavior, rather than prevent violent behavior. The best approach is to learn to sit down, talk calmly with each other, listen carefully, listen with your heart, and work things out in a positive, win-win fashion. If this is difficult to do, take a *time-out* alone by yourself and organize your thinking carefully. It can even help to write down your thoughts so that when you come back to talk rationally with your partner you have clear ideas of what you believe can be done to make things better. Remember: You're on the same team.

- **"Go outside and run around and play football and get rid of all that anger."** This is a simple way of describing *catharsis theory*. This theory holds that you need to vent your anger so that it doesn't build up to dangerous levels. The truth of the matter is that when we become angry, we need to explore ways with our partner to deal positively and effectively with the source of the problem that is bothering us. Going out to play football or running around the block a dozen times may wear a person down physically, but it doesn't do anything to solve the root problem that is causing the individual to be concerned. Doing something that is soothing, such as going for a nature walk, listening to pleasant and calming music or meditation won't solve the problem either. But they *can*

71

help a person calm down enough to think clearly and return to the discussion with one's partner in a more relaxed and friendly mood. Use whatever method that helps you get back to your more reasonable self, but remember, only good communication and conflict resolution skills will *really* solve the root problem.

- **"She's so nice. She never gets angry."** This common belief hinges on the notion that women, somehow, are extra-special and in an important way *not quite human*. It is very clear, however, that everyone—both women and men—get angry. Women have been socialized in our culture to react in a less visibly angry way than men, but women still get angry and they need to find ways to resolve the conflicts they have with their partner. Also, because of their physical limitations, on average, relative to men, women have had to learn less aggressive, nonviolent ways to deal with couple conflicts. Women start arguments, just as men start arguments. When anger leads to pushing and shoving and hitting, women are sometimes the first to get physical. The problem for women is that men are, on average, bigger and stronger, and if the disagreement becomes violent, women are likely to lose. For this simple reason, women have been forced to become more diplomatic in their human relationships, and angry men can learn from women some of these excellent skills in diplomacy if men really want to try. Otherwise, the man is simply being a bully.

- **"If you don't get angry, she'll walk all over you."** Partners often fall into the trap of believing that anger is the only protection they have from their partner. This view of the world turns a couple's relationship into a battleground. Again, the only genuine solution is to view a couple's relationship as a partnership. Your aim is to be best friends, to be members of a two-person team in which both individuals are on the same side and the goal is relative happiness for both.

- **"Well, everybody gets angry. So there!"** Yes, everybody gets angry, because life has its inevitable frustrations and we often don't get what we want. But not everyone acts on their anger, not everyone strikes out from anger, not everyone is violent toward their partner out of anger. Those who want to build positive emotional bonds with their partner find creative and soft-spoken ways to deal with their anger.

- **"I was just kidding."** Many people enjoy putting others down. These put-downs are an expression of anger and a way of lashing out at a partner. Sometimes partners do this in front of other people and, again, say they are just joking. But put-downs are hurtful and humiliating and no one likes to be the victim of a put-down. Relationships in which put-downs are common are likely to be troubled and unhappy relationships.
- **"Anger, actually, can be a good thing."** In a couple relationship, not really. The underlying conflict can be resolved much easier and more quickly by forgetting about anger and getting right to the discussion phase: the talking and listening and building understanding between each other that is necessary if the relationship is to survive and thrive.

To sum it all up, anger is a waste of time and energy and does terrible damage to loving relationships.

"You Always Hurt the One You Love"

As the old song lyric goes, human beings have an amazing ability to hurt each other, especially to hurt the ones to whom we are the closest, the ones we should be treating with the most respect, love and kindness.

Why are we nicer to our boss, our teacher, our school bus driver, the stranger on the corner, than we are to our partner? Why do we reserve our tantrums and foolishness for our partners, our parents, our children?

The answer to these questions is similar to the answer to another very difficult question, "What's the main cause of divorce in the world today?"

And the answer is: "Marriage."

We are nicer to strangers and other acquaintances in our lives because the stakes are so much lower, because there's not much riding on these kinds of relationships, because it's easier to be nice when we aren't locked into the relationship day-after-day, year-after-year, till death do us part. The stakes for a long-term, committed marital relationship are exceptionally high, and we have extremely high expectations in our culture today for marriage. We expect that:

- the marriage will be a stable economic relationship in which the partners always and in every way support each other through financial thick-and-thin;
- the couple, if they choose to have children, will be great parents and love their children as they would love themselves, every minute and all the time;
- the couple will be best friends, loving lovers, and always *up* for each other when they might really be feeling *down*.

These are incredibly high expectations for couples. Too idealistic, really, because no couple has ever succeeded in meeting such high expectations 100% of the time.

One thing we can do to solve this problem is become more realistic about all this. We need to scale down our expectations a bit. In Garrison Keillor's fictitious small town, Lake Wobegon, a fellow named Floyd wanted to build a grocery store for the people of the town. Floyd was a bit leery of setting his sights too high, especially in such a modest village as Lake Wobegon, population a few hundred, so instead of aiming for a *super*market he decided to call his business *Floyd's Pretty-Good Grocery Store*. The expectations for a *super*market were just too high, but a *pretty-good* store seemed just about right to Floyd. In this more modest endeavor he succeeded and he ended up quite happy with the result, and the town did, also.

So why do we always hurt the one we love? Because we are human and because we set impossible goals for ourselves and our marriage partner in our relationship. We are unrealistic and we inevitably fail to meet our elevated expectations, we blame and then try to hurt our partner. If we were to become more realistic about our partnership in Floyd the grocer's term, we might aim for a relationship that is "very good," "very satisfying," or "pretty good."

The Dance of Anger

In her classic book, *The Dance of Anger*, Harriet Goldhor Lerner identified five different styles of anger management that some people use: the *pursuer*, the *distancer*, the *overfunctioner*, the *underfunctioner*, and the *blamer*.

When anxious about a relationship, *pursuers* seek a greater sense of togetherness, want to talk more, want to express their feelings more and are critical of a partner who does not act the same way. This becomes like a dance: When the pursuer moves in closer, the partner moves back and away, the pursuer moves in even closer and closer while the partner keeps trying to retreat to a safer and more comfortable distance. Finally, the pursuer reacts coldly by withdrawing from the dance altogether.

Distancers, on the other hand, are those who want emotional space when stress is high. They are private, self-reliant people who are not inclined to seek help. They find it difficult to show their needs, their vulnerability, their dependency. Partners of distancers describe them as emotionally unavailable, withholding of emotion, and unable to express their feelings. Distancers retreat into their work when a relationship heats up, and may leave altogether if they feel their partner is coming too close. Just imagine how the dance looks when you put a pursuer with a distancer as partners: the pursuer moves in closer and closer and closer as the distancer backs away; then when the pursuer gets frustrated and opts out of the relationship, the distancer feels more comfortable and begins to dance a bit closer—back and forth, back and forth.

Thinking in terms of differences, just as people have different tastes in clothes, in cars, in foods, they also have different habits and likes in terms of closeness and personal space. Dealing successfully with these differences begins with talking about them and identifying the differences; then, the couple can find ways to adjust to each other's differing needs successfully.

A third type of dancer in Lerner's model is called the *underfunctioner.* These types of people cannot seem to get organized in many areas of their life. Under stress the underfunctioner becomes less competent, less able to fulfill his role in the relationship and in the family, and he is eager to have others take over the responsibilities or fill in. Underfunctioners are commonly described as being "the fragile one," "the sick one," "the problem," "the irresponsible one," and so forth. Underfunctioners find it difficult to show their capable and competent side to their partners and feel better when being cared for. They procrastinate about things, waiting until others make decisions for them.

Put an underfunctioner with an *overfunctioner*, and you can see another interesting dance. Overfunctioners tend to be inflexible and when under stress in a relationship are eager to advise, rescue, take charge, fix things. They become uncomfortable when things are not running smoothly and are over eager to jump in and fix everything rather than letting their partner be responsible for herself or himself. Overfunctioners are described as "always reliable," "always prepared," "always capable," and can be a pain in the neck to others. They find it difficult to appear vulnerable and incapable, especially in front of underfunctioners, but deep down overfunctioners often feel inferior and incompetent.

When dancing, overfunctioners swoop in to save the underfunctioner. Overfunctioners are always trying to save the underfunctioner, fix the problem, rescue the underfunctioner from herself or himself. This approach hides the overfunctioner's feelings of inferiority and incompetence. By being overly helpful, the overfunctioner takes away the underfunctioner's right and opportunity to take care of herself and to develop competence and personal strengths. If this type of dance goes on too long, it is usually destined to end unhappily. Something in the relationship snaps: The overfunctioner gets tired of saving the underfunctioner all the time and backs off from this type of relationship and/or the underfunctioner gets tired and feels ashamed of being saved. Eventually, the underfunctioner's abilities start to rise to the surface and the underfunctioner enjoys feeling competent and capable. Sooner or later, the underfunctioner is not an underfunctioner at all, and the overfunctioner is out of a job.

The fifth style of anger management Lerner identifies is the *blamer*. This person has a short fuse and under emotional stress intense feelings rise up. This energy is aimed at changing other people. Blamers hold other people responsible for their feelings of anger, and see others and not themselves as the problem.

Lerner argues that in our society women are encouraged to overfunction in the areas of housework, child care and the management of emotions. In all other areas of life, however, women are commonly socialized to be pursuers and underfunctioners. Men are socialized, on the other hand, to be distancers and overfunctioners (at work but not necessarily at home).

Though most people are likely to demonstrate occasional glimpses of all five styles of anger management, problems are likely to occur when one style dominates a person's generalized patterns of behavior. Lerner explains it this way: "You will have a problem . . . if you are in an extreme position in any one of these categories or if you are unable to observe and change your pattern when it is keeping you angry and stuck."

Do you see anything of yourself in any of these dancers? Does the way you dance together as a couple become a problem for you occasionally? Fortunately, couples can change their dance without having to change their partners. Couples are not doomed to perform the same foolish dance over and over. If as a couple you are not pleased with the way you are dancing together, go out to eat at a quiet and pleasant restaurant and over a nice dinner talk quietly, calmly and in pleasant voices about how you can work better as a team, become unstuck from your dance and create new steps in your dance for the coming years.

Good Advice for Resolving Conflict

There are countless good ideas for effectively resolving conflict between partners. Here are some of our favorites:

- *Focus on the positive aspects of your partner.* And every day let your partner know how much you appreciate her/him. Don't get so terribly wound up about a handful of negative things when the vast majority of things your partner does are commendable. Being habitually negative and dwelling on a partner's faults doesn't work. It leads to an endless cycle of hurt and anger. Being habitually positive does work.
- *Call a time-out.* Parents often use time-outs today when children are getting too wound up. Adults sometimes need a time-out, also. To call a time-out with your partner, simply agree that the situation is getting out of hand and that you will get back together in a half hour or a day or two when the adrenalin has stopped pumping and you can be reasonable.
- *Listen very carefully to your partner. Check out what he or she is saying.* "Let me see if I understand your point here: Are you saying that . . . ?" And then repeat back to your partner what you think she is saying. Many arguments go on needlessly because the partners have no idea what each other is really trying to say.
- *Get to the point. Say what you mean—what you **really** mean.* Besides listening carefully to your partner, make sure that when you speak you are speaking clearly and to the point. Oftentimes, individuals are afraid to say what they are really feeling, so they mask these feelings by attacking their partner on another front. For example, a husband might disagree with how his wife disciplines the children but he does not know how to talk with her about this, so, instead, he becomes very harsh with the kids when they

act up. She then becomes puzzled: "Why is he so angry with little children? What's wrong with him?"

- ***Don't expect your partner to be able to read your mind.*** You may think that *he/she should just know*, but this is not realistic.

- ***Don't humiliate your partner in front of others.*** Shame and embarrassment don't work. The hostilities will simply continue when you're alone together, and the level of anger may be even higher.

- ***The dance of nagging-and-avoidance doesn't work.*** Couples often get into the trap of nagging and avoiding that can easily escalate. Instead of both partners acting like adults, she acts like his mother, nagging him endlessly to do his jobs around the house, and he acts like her son, ignoring her, avoiding her, running away from her. This type of game usually escalates: She nags even more as he refuses to comply. Finally, he is likely to have a temper tantrum, throw things, hit and run away. To get out of this trap, sit down together and admit to each other that this is just a childish game each person is playing. Then, find an adult solution to the problem calmly and rationally. She's not his mother and he's not her son, so it's silly to act like it.

- ***Avoid giving ultimatums.*** Don't get into the game of saying things like, "If you do that again, I will *never, ever . . .*" or "You had better do this *or else!*" This is one of the most heavily confrontational ways people have for arguing with each other, and such a strategy does not cool things down, it tends to heat things up. When people give an ultimatum they are trying to put themselves in an adult position, looking down on the other person, who is supposed to feel like a child. However, the response usually is anger and defiance and the battle escalates.

  In some cases the situation can get so out of hand that the couple is setting themselves up for one person to walk out or even divorce. Don't give ultimatums because you may find yourself doing something you really don't want to do. Ultimatums are the stuff of silly TV shows but in real life they don't work.

- ***Grow up. Calm down. Act like an adult***. Do we sound like your mother here? We're just trying to get your attention. The trouble is, a sad thing often happens when couples and family members get into a conflict situation. Individuals quickly become reduced to behaving like small children, yelling and throwing tantrums. This is precisely how they look to outsiders. This childish behavior may work when we're little kids but as adults we just look foolish to others.

- ***Don't fight dirty. Avoid attacking your partner.*** Conflicts in a relationship are not resolved by attacking each other. Things only become worse. Avoid the temptation to fight dirty, to win by damaging your partner. What good can possibly come from making our loved one feel bad?

- ***Hate begets hate. Love begets love.*** When we are kind to our partner, our partner will be likely to respond with kindness. Similarly, when we are nasty to our partner, we are likely to get nastiness in return.

- ***The silent treatment is fighting dirty.*** When couples get into the game of "What's wrong?"—"Nothing . . . ." the likelihood of successfully resolving the conflict goes down dramatically. The silent treatment does not end a conflict. To end a conflict, the partners have to sit down and listen to each other and talk with each other. In a respectful and kind manner.

- ***Keep sex out of all this.*** Couples often get into the bizarre game of having a big, dramatic and emotional knock-down drag-out fight, followed by tempestuous lovemaking. It is no surprise that this can easily happen, of course, because sex is full of emotion, just as conflicts are full of emotion. However, it is not wise to get into this type of pattern, because it becomes self-reinforcing: If passionate sex follows a big argument, the passionate sex can end up serving as a reinforcer, leading to more big arguments in the future, i.e., "Well, this is an awful argument but I can always hope it will end again in wonderful lovemaking," etc. The problem with this game is that it is way too big a price to pay for sex: If you really want to make love, the road to getting there can be much easier and smoother. Don't pick a fight. Instead, do loving, kind and thoughtful things all day: Listen to your partner and enjoy talking with her or him; help keep the apartment or house clean and orderly; work together preparing a meal; read stories to the kids, do whatever makes the partner's life better. These types of behavior are more happily linked with lovemaking. Don't make the mistake of confusing *anger*-sex and *love*-sex. Love-sex is better.

- *Use "I" statements rather than "you" statements. "I" statements are more gentle and work better.* Blaming each other doesn't work to resolve conflicts effectively and efficiently. It only makes people angry. "You" statements commonly are blame statements: "You shouldn't do that!" or "You always make me so mad!" or "You always sound so stupid when you talk with her!" On the other hand, "I" statements aim toward minimizing blame and working, instead, toward understanding and joint problem solving. For example, if you are upset about your partner talking with another guy, saying "You do that again and I'll pound both of you" isn't likely to have a positive response. If you say, "I worry that you're losing interest in me" might be able to open the doors of discussion, understanding and positive action.

- *Discuss one thing at a time until it is resolved.* When conflicts get out of hand in relationships, the combatants commonly start throwing everything from the past into the argument. Rather than calmly talking about an issue until it is resolved, they bring up one sore point after another until the chance of anything good happening is almost zero. Instead of falling into this trap, pick the most important issue to talk about and save your discussion of other issues until you have resolved the most important issue.

- *It's hard to talk about all this.* When partners talk about how they communicate with each other and how they resolve conflicts between each other, it is called *metacommunication* by experts in couple and family communication. Metacommunication is very difficult to do, of course, because partners have to be very honest, open, straightforward, objective and nonjudgmental during metacommunication phases. The partners have to calm down, talk lovingly and reasonably with each other, and develop solutions rather than keep trying to score points in an argument.

- *Win-Win is much better than Win-Lose.* Loving relationships are not athletic contests nor are they wars between ethnic groups or nations. Loving relationships work well when couples in conflict clearly see that they need to join together and work as a team to find a solution to the issue at hand that is good for both partners. Loving relationships fall apart when the couples get into

Win-Lose types of conflicts, when each is trying to dominate the other.

This approach implies that someone in the household is supposed to be the boss and someone is supposed to be the employee. The problem is that people usually don't love their bosses. They might respect or fear their boss, but they are not particularly likely to love their boss. There is usually an emotional distance between the boss and the employee. And who wants to live in a home that feels more like the workplace?

The reality is, if one partner wins and one partner loses, both are losing. They are losing because a loving relationship between equal partners has broken down. They are acting like they are not playing on the same team but on opposing teams.

- ***Solve the conflict, make things better, create a peaceful and harmonious relationship.*** Long-term loving relationships are much more important than endless bickering. Find a way to love each other and agree on the vast majority of issues. Life is too short to be spent trying to change each other.

- ***Agree to disagree.*** People who love each other simply will never agree on everything. Talk about things that are important to you and have the good sense to stop the debate when it is going nowhere. Loving partners don't always vote for the same presidential candidate. So what?

- ***If you need help, go get help.*** Find a certified marital and family therapist or licensed couples relationship counselor. Researchers have found that the vast majority of couples find counseling sessions helpful. It's not likely to cost much more per session than getting some minor repairs done on your car and, similar to cars, relationships don't fix themselves—the partners have to get involved in the process, sometimes with the help of a skilled professional.

  To learn more about the process of marital and family therapy, and to find a therapist near you, visit the American Association for Marital and Family Therapy website at *www.aamft.org*.

- ***Laugh, have some fun, goof off together.*** We get too serious about life, too tightly wound. Make sure you have some fun with each other. Every day.

- **Be kind to each other.** It's really quite simple when you think about it. Treat your partner with the respect, love and kindness she/he deserves. If we can always strive to be kind to each other, the vast majority of conflicts in our world disappear, as if by magic.

Very Short Stories from Real People

This friend of mine would always get very upset at her husband for never getting her flowers on important occasions, such as anniversaries, birthdays and so forth. Somehow her husband was supposed to automatically do this because her father always did!

I used to get really angry at my wife and I couldn't talk rationally with her, so I would go out running when I was mad. I would run and run and run—many miles—until I was exhausted and all the angry feelings had drained from me. When I came home, it didn't really help much, because I was too tired to sit down and talk with her. So, the problems we were facing weren't solved, I was just too tired to be upset. Finally, after a long time, I learned how to meditate and calm myself down when I was angry, and then when I was calm I still had the energy left to work out solutions to our problems. I don't know why it took me so long to figure this out!

We "had" to start dating again when our kids left home. All of a sudden we had a life again. We looked at each other and decided we needed a time to talk without the TV, so we set up Friday nights as eat-out night. I really prize it and happily give up opportunities to be with other friends that night so that I can be with him ALONE.

I would like to add another dance to the Dance of Anger. I would call it the dance between the nagger and the no-responder. It seems like my husband and I spend too much time doing this dance. It goes like this: I ask him to do something, and he ignores me. So I ask again and he ignores me again. And then I get mad and keep asking and asking and nagging and nagging until both of us hate it. And then he blows up and storms out. I would love to work out a new, happier dance with him.

Discussion Questions

1. Anger is a part of life. What are some strategies that you use to deal positively and effectively with anger?
2. Thinking about Harriet Goldhor Lerner's *Dance of Anger,* are there any dances you do with your partner? Using her model of five types of dances, what kind of dance would you call this? Do you have a unique dance you do that isn't on Lerner's list?
3. It seems like people tend to hurt the ones they love the most. Why do we do this?
4. Why do couples often have sex after a big argument? Does this make sense?
5. What do you do for fun that brings you closer together?
6. Have you expressed kindness recently to your partner? How did you do this? How did your partner react?

Tips for Strengthening Your Relationship

1. Practice maintaining self-control during a disagreement. You're both on the same team, not opposing teams. Work together toward a solution.
2. "No put-downs. This is a safe place." This is a great saying to write out and post on your refrigerator door.
3. Don't waste each other's time by fighting dirty, even though it might be fun.

4. Don't humiliate your partner in front of others. This is one example of fighting dirty. If you want to show emotion in front of others, give your partner a hug and kiss instead.
5. Use sex in a healthy way. Know the difference between *anger* sex and *love* sex.
6. Focus on the positive qualities of your partner, the good things. Be sure to let your partner know when he or she has done something that makes you happy.
7. Be kind to each other.

CHAPTER 7
Friendship, Love and Sexual Intimacy

Few words in the English dictionary have inspired as much discussion, celebration and confusion over the years as the word *love*. In our discussion here we will begin by discussing the notion of *love at first sight*, continue by unraveling the differences between friendship and love, and follow up by discussing eight different types of loving relationships. From there we will move on to a look at emotional intimacy: how emotional intimacy compares to sexual intimacy; how emotional intimacy can be developed in a relationship; and how to maintain emotional intimacy in a marriage through the passage of time.

Love at First Sight

Some couples will tell you that it was love at first sight. Some will say that it was love at first sight for one but not the other. Some will say it was infatuation or desire at first sight or joke that it was *lust* at first sight, but not love. Some will say that they were aware of each other for many months or many years but did not become interested in each other as a partner until much later. Some will say they were just friends and the friendship developed slowly over time into love.

In other descriptions of how couples get together, we learn of those who were in bed with each other on the first date, and of others who did not make love until they were married. Some will say that just because they were in bed didn't mean love had anything to do with it at all. Some will say they *fell in love* quickly but *grew into love* slowly over time. The stories partners tell about how they met and how love developed in the relationship are fascinating and remarkably unique, but there are some common patterns.

Our view is that infatuation, romance and sexual desire play a great part early in a relationship. Human behavior, by its very nature, is rooted in biology and our bodies have enormous control over our thinking and our behavior. Watch a nature program on television and it is quite easy to see similarities between the birds or bees or elk or cheetahs in their sexual behavior and the sexual behavior of humans. We might aspire as a species to a higher and more noble order of behavior, but the fact is that we often fall remarkably far from the mark.

Looking at human relationships from this relatively realistic perspective, we conclude that *falling in love* is easy but *staying in love* is much more difficult. Our bodies make falling in love a relatively simple prospect, but the area of our brain that controls rational, clear and logical thinking has to be involved through the months and years if we are going to be able to make this love grow into something deeper and more lasting.

Friendship Compared to Love

Love causes an enormous amount of happiness in the world and an enormous amount of pain. In an ideal world, human beings would take the time needed to create a loving relationship with each other. The foundation of this relationship would be friendship. In our ongoing research on *great marriages*, we are seeing that for many couples the best definition of a great marriage is that the partners are *best friends*.

How do friendship and love compare? Keith E. Davis, a psychologist, has done perhaps the most creative research in this area. He has found, basically, that love is friendship with a few added components.

Friendship develops between two individuals who view each other as equals. There are eight important elements to a successful friendship:

- *Enjoyment.* Friends like to be with each other. Though they have occasional disagreements, they tend to get along very well, most of the time.
- *Acceptance.* Friends accept each other for who they are and don't waste much time trying to change each other.
- *Trust.* Friends can depend on each other to act in the other person's best interest.
- *Respect.* Friends hold each other in high regard, believing that each has good judgment and considerable ability in life.

- *Mutual assistance.* Friends help each other when called upon and are there for each other in difficult times.
- *Confiding in each other.* Friends talk with each other about their experiences in life and are comfortable expressing their feelings.
- *Understanding.* Friends know a great deal about each other's values, beliefs, feelings and behaviors. They are open with each other and this openness leads to understanding.
- *Spontaneity.* Friends can *be real* with each other and don't have to play games or try to be something they really aren't.

Friendship, we have seen, is like love but love has extra components.

And what are the added components? Davis argues that if you have the eight components of friendship and pair them with two more broad components, *passion* and *caring,* you have love. He explains these two extra components this way:

- *Passion* includes fascination for the other person, sexual desire and a desire for exclusiveness. The individual in love is preoccupied with the loved one, cannot stop thinking about the other person and wants to be with the person all the time. Sexual desire is the need to touch each other, hold each other and make love. But some couples may not engage in sexual intercourse until after marriage because of their religious beliefs, moral reasons or practical considerations. Exclusiveness is the need to have the loved one to yourself and no one else. In most cases this is a relatively healthy need, but, of course, it can get out of hand for a number of reasons. For example, extreme jealousy can be damaging to both partners and has to be controlled. Also, individuals come to a relationship not truly as individuals but as a part of an extended family. This family of origin should not be cast aside by passion. People also come with friends and jobs and activities that they love and these should not be sacrificed to passion either.
- *Caring* has two components: being an advocate for one's partner and giving one's utmost to the partner. Those in love are champions and advocates for their loved ones, defending and supporting their partner, through good times and bad. Giving one's utmost is easy for people who are in love; on some occasions they give to the point of self-sacrifice.

The loss of a friend, or especially the loss of a loved one, can be a devastating experience. We all are familiar with stories of elderly men or women who withered and died soon after the death of their partner. Illness and even suicide can follow the loss. Though love is more than friendship, both kinds of human relationships are very important in people's lives.

The Love Triangle: Eight Types Of Love Relationships

Another useful way of thinking about love has been developed by psychologist Robert J. Sternberg and his colleagues. The researchers call this the *love triangle*, with the three sides labeled *commitment*, *intimacy* and *passion*. If you can't see the love triangle in your mind, just take a pencil and draw a triangle, then label each of the three sides:

- *Commitment* is a sense of attachment to another person. Commitment takes time to develop. The process begins slowly and increases at a faster rate if the relationship is a positive one. The expressed level of commitment individuals have for each other increases as the relationship moves through various stages: dating to engagement, engagement to marriage. Commitment is also expressed when partners stay faithful to each other, in spite of temptation, and when the relationship endures through very difficult times.

- *Intimacy* includes the sharing of feelings and providing emotional support for each other. Emotionally intimate partners usually have a high level of self-disclosure in the relationship and are not afraid of talking about their beliefs and feelings openly. Intimacy increases gradually over time as the partners feel closer to each other and the relationship matures. Few couples are likely to share everything about themselves—most everyone seems to need some private space in life—but in a well-developed, positive relationship most areas are open for discussion. When we open up, sharing our thoughts and feelings, and are treated with respect and kindness, our trust for each other grows and a strong emotional bond is formed. It may seem strange but by expressing feelings of weakness and vulnerability, we gain support and strength from each other and the relationship is strengthened.

- *Passion,* expressed by kissing, touching, hugging and sexual intercourse, is linked with physiological arousal of the body. Passionate feelings are indescribable reactions; they build up quickly and also can disappear quickly. Passion, generated by chemical interactions in our bodies, can be a wonderful feeling. There is no denying it. Passion makes the world go round. But it needs to be recognized that passion also can have a drug-like effect on us and for some can turn into a serious and damaging addiction. In some cases when passion has run its course a person can feel irritable and depressed.

Summing up, Sternberg's love triangle includes commitment, intimacy and passion. Now, when you combine these various components of love in different ways, Sternberg believes that you end up with eight different kinds of love: non-love, liking, infatuation, empty love, romantic love, fatuous love, companionate love and consummate love. Let's look at each type of love in more detail:

- *Non-love* is the absence of all three components, commitment, intimacy and passion.
- *Liking* is a type of relationship in which there is intimacy but no commitment or passion.
- *Infatuation* is a state involving passion without commitment or intimacy.
- *Empty love* is defined by Sternberg as commitment without intimacy or passion.
- *Romantic love* has intimacy and passion without commitment.
- *Fatuous love* is a state in which the couple has become committed to each other because of their passionate feelings but they have not had the time to develop genuine intimacy with each other.
- *Companionate love* describes many couples who have been married for several years. The relationship is high on commitment and intimacy and low on the passion that may have fueled their early marriage.
- *Consummate love* is a complete form of love and the goal of most couples, according to Sternberg, for it combines all three components: commitment, intimacy and passion.

Using Sternberg's love triangle, think about your own experiences with love. How would you label each of them? Why?

Love, Jealousy and Abuse

Jealousy is a common feeling for both men and women. When we are jealous we tend to want to have our loved one all to ourselves, exclusively. Competition from others causes jealous partners to feel insecure, hurt and angry. Extreme feelings of jealousy can lead to extreme behavior, and partners are sometimes abused physically and emotionally by the jealous party.

Some couples agree to try to avoid situations that can spark jealous feelings. This can be very difficult, of course, when you work with people of the other sex or even when you have friendships with people of the same sex that you would like to maintain. Some partners, especially women, feel as if their male partner is overly-controlling and feel almost trapped by his jealous feelings. They try to reassure their partner that he has nothing to worry about. Some men, however, cannot seem to control these feelings.

Couples should talk openly and honestly about jealousy and what makes each partner jealous. They should make a genuine effort to come to some reasonable compromise in regard to these issues. This is much easier to do than trying to deal with a situation in which jealousy has spiraled out of control.

Individuals are likely to be somewhat different in their feelings about jealousy: Some individuals might be more quick to feel jealous than others, having less tolerance for relationships with other people; some individuals might be more jealous about the partner having a friendship with a member of *the other* sex, while some might be equally jealous about an outside friendship with *either* sex; also, some individuals are especially jealous about sexual involvements outside the couple relationship, while others feel more threatened by outside friendships that may, or may not, be sexual in nature.

A good way to prevent problems from developing is to try to personally avoid social situations in which you might be tempted to enjoy the company of other people who would make your partner jealous, and situations that might entice you into behavior with others that you could end up seriously regretting. An affair, either an emotional affair or a sexual affair, can be disastrous to a marriage. Some family therapists argue that the vast majority of divorces are related to an extramarital affair.

If you are not ready to settle down and end your period of dating (shopping) around, it is unwise to try to hold on to a partner and expect her or him to remain committed to you while you are still interested in being with other people. This behavior is simply not fair to your partner, nor is it fair to new people with whom you would like to enjoy spending time.

Because our feelings about jealousy are all so individualistic, it is important to discuss this issue in an effort to prevent serious problems later on. A few thoughts that might prove useful during your discussion:

- Jealousy is a pretty normal feeling, in the sense that many people feel jealousy on occasion.
- If you don't ever feel jealous, it might be because you believe your partner is very trustworthy, or you might simply not care all that much about your partner.
- Jealousy crosses the borderline into abusive behavior when the jealous person loses all trust for her or his partner and tries to control every aspect of the person's life.
- If your anger is getting out of control and you harbor violent thoughts toward your partner and her or his friends, it is time to find a therapist who can help bring rational thinking back into your discussions with each other.
- For loving relationships to work, honesty is clearly the best policy.

Sexual Intimacy Compared to Emotional Intimacy

When people talk about being sexually intimate, they are usually talking about behavior that involves sexual behaviors of various levels, including touching and stroking of the genitals, and sexual intercourse.

On the other hand, to be emotionally intimate or close with another person involves honest, open and straightforward communication; it involves sharing our most important thoughts and feelings with each other and gaining comfort and strength from these dialogues. Emotional intimacy is the kind of intimacy that genuine friends have with each other. It tends to be relatively stable and can last a lifetime.

Sex sometimes goes hand-in-hand with emotional intimacy, but sometimes people engage in sexual behavior without any feelings of closeness and emotional connection at all. Sexual intimacy and emotional intimacy are very different from each other and individuals should not get them confused.

If a couple can achieve both sexual intimacy, which is relatively easy, and emotional intimacy, which is relatively difficult to achieve, a strong and enduring bond is likely to be developing between the partners.

How do you explain the differences between sexual intimacy and emotional intimacy? Have there been times when you have had one without the other? Have there been times when you have had both simultaneously?

Developing Emotional Intimacy

Couples face many challenges together in life. As they struggle through these challenges, they learn more and more about each other. If they are skillful in meeting these challenges, their sense of emotional closeness is likely to deepen over time. Developing emotional intimacy is a complex process that can take several years. Older couples will likely tell you that the process has continued throughout their long-term marriage.

David H. Olson, Amy K. Olson-Sigg and Peter Larson conducted a national survey of more than 50,000 married couples. They wanted to identify the differences between happy and unhappy couples. The researchers classified 20,675 couples as happily married and 20,590 couples as unhappily married based on their scores on a marital satisfaction scale. A middle group of about 10,000 couples were not included in either group because their marital satisfaction scales were moderate or because one partner scored high and one scored low. Those who were judged to be happily married had developed emotional intimacy in their relationship. The researchers found that emotional intimacy for couples is especially tied to success in eight challenging areas of their relationship:

- *Communication skills.* Couples who are good at communicating with each other are likely to develop an emotional bond with each other.

- *Conflict resolution skills.* Feelings of emotional intimacy are linked to a couple's ability to find win-win solutions to their inevitable conflicts in life.
- *Sexual relations.* Satisfying sexual expression for both partners can build emotional intimacy.
- *Couple flexibility.* A couple's ability to adapt to life's inevitable stressors and make necessary changes to meet these difficulties head-on is linked to the development of emotional intimacy. Couples who work together during hard times are likely to feel closer to each other than those who work at cross-purposes.
- *Couple closeness.* A common complaint of many couples is the difficulty finding time for each other in a busy world. Couples who demonstrate the importance of their partnership by making time for each other every day are likely to feel closer than those who let the many concerns and cares of the world pull them apart.
- *Personal compatibility.* Things we like about our partner strengthen the bond of intimacy we are trying to develop in our relationship. Positive traits include friendliness, optimism, honesty, kindness, the ability to communicate, reliability and many others. What are the personality traits that make your partner attractive to you? And, what personality traits do you have that make you attractive to your partner? How can these traits be strengthened?
- *Good relationships with family and friends.* Positive relationships with the extended family make it much easier for the couple relationship to flourish. Strained relationships outside the marriage put pressure on the couple. Though a strong partnership can withstand enormous difficulties brought on by troubles in the families of origin, problems with the extended family do cause stress for many couples. Similarly, friendships with other couples who are basically happy with each other are important to develop. Having couple friends to talk about couple ups and downs can be very helpful in developing emotional intimacy, because we learn very quickly that every partnership faces difficulties and we learn how generally healthy and happy partnerships deal with adversity successfully.
- *Shared spiritual values.* It has been said that human beings find it easier to argue about their religious faiths than to actually practice

them. Couples who find a set of broad spiritual values that they can share without fighting over the details are more likely to develop the emotional closeness so vital for a strong marriage. If you get in a power struggle over who is right and who is wrong, you both are likely to lose in the end, for the relationship will be severely damaged. Emotional intimacy does not dictate that the partners agree with each other on everything. Emotional intimacy does dictate, however, that the partners trust each other and feel safe and comfortable enough with each other to share their religious and spiritual beliefs without getting into an argument.

Maintaining Emotional Intimacy Over Time

Couples find soon enough that the initial excitement and passion so common in relationships in their early stages can disappear as time passes. The thrill of getting to know another person emotionally and sexually is a wonderful process and we all hope at some time in our lives that it would last forever. In truth, however, the thrill does disappear as life inevitably gets back into its normal routine. School, jobs, in-laws, broken-down cars, children—whatever the challenges couples face, these challenges drain energy away from the initial thrill of love. This has led some observers to say that the long-term, routinized process of marriage by its very nature can lead to difficulties.

And yet, countless couples maintain emotional intimacy over time, and they do this by making sure that their partnership is the most important asset they have in their lives together. When we realize that a strong bond between the partners is the glue that holds our life together, we invest time, energy and creativity every day into maintaining that bond.

It is, indeed, the best investment we can make.

Very Short Stories from Real People

There weren't lots of fireworks at the beginning. I thought he was kind of a clumsy nerd because he had a cast on his wrist from a bicycle accident. Dave and I lived in the same dorm before we started dating. It wasn't a love at first sight. As we got to know each other, it grew into love. Two years later we were married.

94

For my husband it was love at first sight, but it wasn't for me. I wasn't looking for a relationship, but he was. His over-infatuation was driving me nuts. We had to work through the over-attentiveness. I needed my space.

My husband skipped his uncle's funeral to attend our 30-year class reunion because he was jealous that I'd be spending time with old college guy friends. When I was in college, these were the guys who I hung around with, except when I was out on a date with him. What really got him was when I would even skip class to play tennis with these guys.

I have no idea what to do. My mother still wants to hold on tight to me, and my wife doesn't like it at all. If I choose my wife, I lose my mother. If I choose my mother, I lose my wife. Why can't these two women get along?

When Jason and I were working at camp, we weren't spending much time together, so we decided that we would eat together routinely, no matter what the time. Nine years later, we have maintained our dinner time together as a couple. We still make this a priority. It helps us maintain our emotional intimacy.

Discussion Questions

1. How did you first meet your partner, and what were your first thoughts?
2. Do you believe in love at first sight? Explain.

3. How do you describe the differences between friendship and love?
4. What makes you jealous?
5. How do you find a healthy balance between your friends and your partner? What if the friend is of the other sex?
6. How do you maintain emotional intimacy over time?

Tips for Strengthening Your Relationship

1. Marriages cannot be entirely based on passion. Passion comes and goes and has to be nurtured over time.
2. Be respectful of your partner's feelings of insecurity when you are with people of the other sex, or even your friends of the same sex.
3. Don't carry your feelings to the extreme and deny your partner's need to have friendships outside the marriage.
4. Sexual intimacy and emotional intimacy are very different from each other. Don't get them confused.
5. Find a set of broad spiritual values that you can share without fighting over the details. This will help develop the emotional closeness so vital to a strong marriage.

CHAPTER 8

His Work and Her Work:
Roles Partners Play
And Power in the Relationship

For centuries, America has been engaged in a vigorous and emotional discussion of the alleged differences between men and women. Throughout our history and even today, men have been seen as strong, tough, hard-driving. Women, on the other hand, have been stereotyped as kind, gentle, emotional and eager to connect with other people. Putting males and females into convenient boxes makes it easy for us to talk about them as groups, but when we look closely we find countless individuals that just don't fit into the stereotypic boxes. Tough, aggressive women and tender, gentle men are examples of exceptions. The boxes we put people in do not help us explain the world very well, and if we get carried away with these stereotypes in our relationships with each other, these boxes can cause a great deal of damage.

Perhaps the biggest problem that this kind of simplistic thinking causes in our culture is that we assign roles to men and women based on anatomy alone, and then we give power to men based on anatomical differences rather than skills and interests. A couple's argument might look like this:

> He [joking]: *Let me understand this clearly then. I have to change oil in the car and tar the leak in the roof because I have a penis. Is that the logic?*
> She [laughing along with his joke]: *Yes. And I have to cook every meal and clean the toilet because I have breasts.*

Stated in this twisted way, it becomes clear that we need to think about the roles partners play in a couple relationship in a more reasonable fashion. When we fall into the trap of stereotypic-thinking sets for men and women, we often give men the more exciting, interesting, influential and well-paying roles, and this leads to an imbalance in power between men and women. The trouble is, when one partner has an unequal share of the power, the relationship can suffer; resentment can grow to poison the love that the couple once shared.

How does this translate into the daily lives of couples? David H. Olson, Amy Olson-Sigg and Peter Larson found in their study of more than 50,000 couples in the U.S. that there were five major role relationship issues many couples faced:

- 49% had a concern about the unfair division of housework.
- 44% believed that housework was based on traditional roles rather than individual interests.
- 44% believed that the husband was not as willing to adjust as much as the wife.
- 43% disagreed about whether the wife should work outside the home when the children are young.
- 40% disagreed that both worked to maintain an egalitarian or equal relationship.

If we are to increase mutual respect between partners, which is the foundation for a loving and caring relationship, we need to find ways to distribute power, authority, influence—and housework—more equally and fairly in the home. Couples who do so are more likely to experience a happy marriage.

Male Traits and Female Traits

The Gallup Organization has conducted both national and international surveys that shed light on how people around the world think about the differences and similarities between men and women. In the American study, Gallup asked people which traits were "more true of men" and which traits were "more true of women." Gallup found that in describing males, the three top-ranked descriptors stated by both men and women, in order, were: (1) *aggressive,* (2) *courageous* and (3) *ambitious.* Similarly, in describing females, five top-ranked descriptors stated by both men and women, in order, were: (1) *emotional,* (2) *affectionate,* (3) *talkative,* (4) *patient* and (5) *creative.* Three traits used often to describe both men and women, but in different orders for each, were: *ambitious, easygoing* and *intelligent*.

Gallup also surveyed people in 22 countries and found conventional stereotypes in these countries that were similar to the ones in the U.S. Women, when compared to men, were seen worldwide as being more *affectionate, emotional, talkative* and *patient*. In America, 76% of the people in the survey said women were the more affectionate sex, while 6% said men were; and 88% of Americans said women were more emotional while only 4% said that of men.

The Gallup international survey found that no trait was seen as exclusively a male or female domain, but the trait considered as most likely to be male was *aggressiveness*. In China, 81% identified aggressiveness as most common among men, while only 3% said it was most characteristic of women, a difference of 78 points. In the U.S. the margin on aggression for men compared to women was 58 points, while in Canada and Great Britain the margin was 60 points.

People worldwide clearly see patterns in how males and females behave. Are these very conventional ways of thinking about men and women around the world true? Probably. The evidence from the Gallup surveys indicates that there are generalized differences between groups of males and females in terms of various behaviors. But differences between groups of people do not describe individuals. In other words, just because many men are aggressive does not mean *all* men are aggressive *or even should be* aggressive. Just because many women are talkative does not imply that some men who are talkative should not be, or that if they are, they have assumed a feminine characteristic.

As the late John Davidson, a wise botany professor at the University of Nebraska–Lincoln would say, "If your theory says that all clovers have three leaves and you find a clover with four leaves, *it ain't the clover that's wrong!*"

Traditional and Contemporary Views Of Male and Female Roles

The traditional view of roles for males and females in the family was expressed by sociologist Talcott Parsons in the 1950s and 1960s. The so-called *normal* family for Parsons included a husband, a wife and children. Husbands were to be *instrumental* in their behavior, the breadwinner and take-charge leader of the family. Wives were to be expressive, to serve as the emotional foundation of the family, caring for, nurturing and comforting the husband and children. These roles did not overlap with each other in Parsons' thinking, but rather were separate: Husbands had their distinct role in the family, and wives had their distinct role.

Fast-forward American culture 50 years. Today, there are still many couples who have chosen to be traditional in their approach to family life. But, the percentage of nontraditional or contemporary families has increased dramatically. When people use the term *normal family*, they often smile or even smirk, because there is no one-size-fits-all type of family that is generally agreed to be best for everyone, counter to Parsons' beliefs a half-century ago. Instead, *diversity is the new normal*. There are many types or structures of couple and family relationships, and freedom of choice is widely recognized and desirable.

Of course, there are still many two-parent, traditional families today. There are also stable and happy single-parent families, stepfamilies, healthy-functioning families with gay and lesbian parents, couples who have chosen not to have children, extended families with grandfathers, grandmothers and adult siblings connected, and families made up of people who are not related by birth or marriage but who have chosen to be together because they care for each other and value their relationships so much. These types of families have been described as *fictive kin, chosen families* or *symbolic families*, to name just a few terms used. These are the people in our lives we sometimes describe as being "just like family to me." All these types of families are not seen as superior or inferior to Parsons' traditional family. Rather, they are seen as workable family patterns for countless people. In the case of families, one size or type does not fit all.

In Australia during 1999-2000, Judi Geggie, John DeFrain, Sharon Hitchcock and Simone Silberberg interviewed and surveyed 690 families who volunteered for the study and believed they were strong, happy, satisfied and loving families. These so-called *strong families* were asked to describe the type of family they lived in: "Who are the people in your family?" The fascinating finding was that besides traditional, two-parent families in Australia who believed they were strong families, there were 31 other types of families also described by the people in the study because these families felt they were happy together. Many participants in the research insisted on including their dog or cat in the list of members of their family! The researchers in the Australian study concluded that *strong families come in all shapes and sizes and types.* And, as we have said before, it's really not about the structure of the family, but rather how the family, whatever structure, functions. The key is that it is composed of people who love and care for each other.

The Decline of Male Dominance And the Rise of Equality

A lot has happened in the world since Talcott Parsons wrote about so-called normal families in the 1950s and 1960s. The widespread use of contraception has led to women having smaller families. In spite of current economic turmoil, families are relatively prosperous when compared to the generations of our grandparents and great-grandparents. These factors have contributed to increased educational opportunities for young women, who are more likely today to be able to afford a college education. The college degree increases the possibility of getting a good job. Money is power in American society, for better and worse, and when women began making significant contributions to the family income, they gained power in relationship to their husbands.

This new-found sense of power is exhibited in many ways in a couple relationship: Partners don't have to stay with mates who are emotionally, physically or sexually abusive, or ones who are addicted to alcohol or other drugs. It is likely wives have gained more of a voice in the home, free to offer their opinions about how the household is run. Rather than one vote in the home—the husband's vote—two votes are now common and in the case of a tie vote, wives have lots of room for negotiation with their husbands about decisions that are made. In the bedroom there have been changes, also. Sex for many wives in the past may have been something to endure rather than enjoy, but today with increased freedom from serial pregnancy, women have discovered the joy of sex. The old double standard that allowed men more sexual and social freedom is in decline as women claim more freedom for themselves.

All these developments have led to a decline in the power of men and the rise in male/female equality.

Housework in Many Ways Is Still
A Woman's Domain

In many ways, women's lives have changed more than men's lives since the 1950s. The number of women working outside the home even upon the arrival of children in their lives, has increased dramatically in the past several decades. Women have adapted to the workplace very well and are changing the so-called working world in many ways. Many observers argue that men have not been adapting as quickly in terms of housework and caring for children. However, some men may take on responsibilities that could not have been imagined in decades past.

The argument goes this way: When a mother leaves home and finds a job, she is taking on extra responsibilities in life, and the hours of work she puts in each week increase dramatically. But, when she comes home she often finds that her male partner is reluctant to add to his workload by doing housework or argues that he is just not good at doing these kinds of things. Men also argue that they contribute at home by doing men's jobs: maintaining the cars, fixing electronic gadgets in the home, doing physically demanding work outside, and so forth.

The researchers who study how people spend their time in the home and issues surrounding the division of labor between men and women tend to side with mothers and see a clear imbalance: Mothers seem to put in more hours of work at home than fathers, both in housework and in caring for children. Other researchers note that fathers tend to put in more hours on their job than mothers, on average, but all things considered, mothers appear to work more hours than fathers in an average week.

The key issue, then, seems to be individuals' perceptions of fairness more than simply the number of hours worked. If one of the partners perceives a definite imbalance in the workload, negotiations need to begin before resentful feelings poison the relationship.

What do you feel about how the workload is balanced in your partnership? What does your partner feel about this? If you are a mom who has chosen to stay at home, how does this affect the workload balance in your relationship? Do the expectations change for a stay-at-home dad?

International Perspectives on Male/Female Roles

Women do more housework and child care in the home than men, and a good guess for why this is true is because men have more power in the world. Is this something that has happened because of human biology and natural forces, or is it influenced more by culture and tradition?

The classic answer to the age-old question of male and female roles was given by Margaret Mead, perhaps the most famous cultural anthropologist in the world in the 20th century. Mead was interested in the concepts of *maleness* and *femaleness* when she visited three traditional tribes in New Guinea in the 1930s: the Arapesh, the Mundugumor and the Tchambuli. The tribes all lived on the same large island but were separated by extremely difficult terrain—steep mountains, fast-flowing streams, rain forests—and so intercultural contact was limited.

Americans, as we have seen, tend to traditionally see females as gentle and unaggressive. Among the Arapesh both women and men were not aggressive, and their behavior in this regard would be described as feminine by many Americans. Among the Mundugumor tribe, living nearby, both women and men were aggressive in a way that Americans would describe as being traditionally masculine. In both tribes, males and females tended to behave very similarly in terms of aggression or nonaggression.

The third tribe Mead visited, the Tchambuli, were sex-typed in regard to aggression, but in a fascinating way for Americans: Tchambuli women were independent and aggressive, and Tchambuli men were gentle and sensitive.

Mead concluded from these observations in her 1935 book, *Sex and Temperament in Three Primitive Societies,* that human biology does not necessarily dictate how we behave. Instead, she decided that human cultural rules and traditions influence to a considerable degree how we behave.

Mead's work sparked a discussion in America and worldwide that has not ended yet nor is it likely to ever reach a conclusion, because the discussion and the controversy are too much fun for everyone. One study by psychologist David Buss is a good example of another important perspective in the discussion of maleness and femaleness. Buss and his colleagues created a questionnaire to be used around the world, asking people to describe their ideal mate. Five categories were included: earning capacity, industriousness, youth, physical attractiveness and chastity.

Buss collected data from 37 groups of men and women in 33 different societies.

The researchers found that even though the participants in the study came from many different geographical and cultural areas, consistent patterns emerged. Females placed more value on wealth and ambition, and males were more interested in signs of youth and fertility. A mate who was a "good financial prospect" was more important to females in 36 of 37 groups, and "good looks" were more important to males than females in all 37 groups in the study.

The Gallup Organization surveyed men and women in 22 countries around the world regarding gender roles in the family. Residents of nearly two-thirds of the countries believed that their society favors men over women. Countries in greatest agreement with this belief included: Germany (76%), Iceland (76%), France (76%), the United States (73%), and Great Britain (72%). In seven countries the consensus leaned toward the belief that men and women are treated equally: El Salvador (63%), China (53%), and Thailand (52%).

What does this all mean for a couple hoping to achieve a strong, loving and caring relationship? It means that as a couple, you would find it useful to talk about your personal beliefs regarding roles in the partnership:

- Do you each have specific roles?
- Do you share some roles?
- Why have you arranged your life together this way?
- Does it seem fair to each of you?
- Are there some things you would like to change?
- How can you work together to make these changes possible so that your partnership will be even stronger?

Power in Families

Throughout human history, from our darkest past to this very day, the struggle for power has been a major theme. Nations struggle to gain power over each other and struggle to defend their freedoms against dominance by other nations. Ethnic majorities defend their advantages of being in the majority against efforts by minority groups to gain a piece of the pie. And in families in which we are uncomfortable talking about it, power is also an ever-present reality whether we like it or not.

Men, for the most part, have been dominant over women in the family through the millennia. The natural advantages men have over women—size, muscle structure, aggressiveness—have carried the day for men for a long, long time and in many households today, some males still rule by the threat of force and violence.

The world, however, is slowly changing, and in American families most struggles for power are waged more subtly. Violence inflicted upon a spouse may be relatively rare, but the competition for power and control between partners is very common. This is true because we are all individuals with unique thoughts and feelings about our world and how it should be organized and maintained. These unique perceptions come into conflict frequently behind closed doors.

It is likely that the use of brute force in families has declined over the passage of time. But power still is distributed to the individuals who have significant resources. In a marriage these resources are likely to include money, educational level and occupational prestige. The more resources a person has, the more power he or she is likely to have. Traditionally, men have had more of these resources in the average marriage, but as we have seen, women's resources have increased dramatically in the past several decades.

Interestingly enough, in households where both partners work outside the home and those in which the woman makes more money than the man, researchers have found that women's perceived power has not increased proportionally to the increase in their occupation and job status.

Why? The researchers argue that in these cases, women apparently have been less willing to take advantage of their increased resources. Something apparently is holding them back.

Some observers have argued that power in families is much more than simply money, educational level and occupational prestige. People discover value in many things: a beautiful smile, the sun shining on golden hair, a sense of humor, the ability to fix the car. Or, as one father described it:

> Think of the power of a two-year-old, screeching at the top of her lungs in a grocery store. The world stops as your mind struggles for a solution to the problem; all eyes in the store look demandingly at you, the parent, to do something. And what can you do? Smother the kid? No. You grab her up in

105

your arms and rush out of the store to the car, hiding your
shame.

So, who had the so-called power in this situation: 200-pound Dad or
22-pound Melissa?

In the classic description of power patterns in marriage, P.G. Herbst
argued that power is distributed in four basic ways:

- *The husband-dominant marriage* in which the husband makes
  most of the decisions alone, while the wife decides a few things
  alone.
- *The wife-dominant marriage* in which the wife makes most of the
  decisions alone, while the husband decides a few things alone.
- *The shared-authority approach* in which most decisions are made
  jointly while a few decisions are made by the husband alone or the
  wife alone.
- *The relatively autonomous marriage,* in which the husband decides
  many things alone, the wife decides many things alone, and the
  couple jointly decides a few things.

What kind of power pattern has evolved in your partnership? Is this the
kind of relationship you really want? How would you like to change
things?

How Can We Change Male/Female Roles In a Family?

If one or both partners are not happy with the way roles and responsibilities
are distributed in the relationship, it is important that the couple sit down
and quietly and calmly create a new way of living together. For example,
one partner brings up the fact that he or she feels overwhelmed by life.
This is done with an "I" message: "I feel so overworked and tired. I just
can't get everything done. I need some help." The discussion can then
move on to what jobs can be changed, what jobs can be eliminated and
what jobs can be shared. The discussion might also focus on personal
expectations that have roots in each partner's family of origin: "I know
this is the way it was done in your Mom and Dad's family, but in my own
family it was very different . . . ." At the end of the discussion the couple

can agree to make necessary changes and then revisit the issues in a couple weeks to see how things are going.

In many respects, the old way of thinking about power in life and in families is obsolete. Rather than thinking about life as a continuous struggle for dominance over each other, we need to think about marriage as a team effort in which both partners are working together to increase each other's happiness.

Forget what you learned on television. Political parties have nothing to teach couples about happy marriage. Competing businesses and countries struggling against each other also have nothing to teach you.

The way to change male/female roles in a family must come from the heart: from a genuine desire to serve each other's best interests and needs. Old ways of thinking about power and leadership focused on a hierarchy—a top-down model. These ways may have some advantages if you're in a giant, enormously complex corporation or the military, but in the intimate environment of the family they are unnecessary and counter-productive.

Academic researchers working in the field of leadership studies often talk positively about so-called *servant leadership*, a model of leadership in which the job of the head of the group is to work to increase the general well-being and happiness of the group. The leader's role is not to feather his own nest, but to advance the interests of everyone in the group.

A model of servant leadership in a two-parent family would include parents who both have important capabilities and responsibilities to serve the needs of the total family. As the children grow in age and capabilities, they also would gain more responsibility in helping maintain the well-being of the total family. The benefits to the servant leaders in this model are the same benefits that everyone else gains in the family: a feeling of connection, comfort, well-being and satisfaction, in particular, from knowing that he or she has served the family well.

Mutual Respect Increases Marital Happiness

Mutual respect between two people implies that they see each other to be of equal value. Not the same in everything, by any means, for we are all different, all unique. Instead, the partners see they are equals in terms of value: Each brings important gifts to the partnership and the family and these gifts are of considerable value to all.

The biggest problem with traditional approaches to couple and family relationships is that individuals lower on the totem pole are likely to feel under-valued and disrespected. David H. Olson, Amy Olson-Sigg and Peter Larson demonstrated the danger in their national survey of more than 50,000 couples that we mentioned earlier. The researchers divided the couples into two groups: those who perceived their relationship as traditional and those who perceived their relationship as more contemporary (an equal or egalitarian relationship). Among the egalitarian relationships, 81% of the couples agreed that their marriage was happy and only 19% described their marriage as unhappy. Among the traditional couples, 18% agreed that their marriage was happy and 82% said the marriage was unhappy. This is clearly a critical issue in the lives of the couple.

What are you thinking right now?

Very Short Stories from Real People

He: She's always so manipulative. She always tries to pull a fast one on me. She sweet talks me and tries to trip me up. Why can't she just come out and say it. Why can't she be more straightforward? Be more like a man?

She: What am I supposed to do? You're so big and get angry so easily and start huffing and puffing and yelling. I'm afraid of you! I've got to figure out subtle ways to change your mind on things because you're so stubborn and aggressive. You don't fight fair at all.

A young architect and her husband made the conscious decision that he would stay at home to care for their child in a city where child care was at a premium. This decision allowed him to pursue an interest in music while caring for the young boy and the mother no longer had to worry that her son was not being cared for properly, enabling her to focus on her job.

Issues of power become more complex in families in which stepparents are involved. My husband and I have worked out our shared roles as marriage partners; however, we often have conflicting parental expectations, making some decisions more difficult to agree on. In the end, right or wrong, I usually have the final word by default since the children are "mine." That means I also bear the total responsibility for an outcome with unfavorable results because I made a wrong parenting choice.

My husband has always made less money since I was able to pursue a master's degree and find better paying jobs. His staying home was a win-win situation for us as he was able to pursue his carpentry as a self-employed person. This also made it easier for us to manage the children; he was free to take off work when they were sick or go to their games and activities.

Discussion Questions

1. Do you think housework and child care are fairly distributed in your home? If not, how could you work together to find a solution to this dilemma?
2. Regarding your couple relationship:

    *   Do you each have specific roles that you play in your life together?
    *   Do you share some roles?
    *   Why have you arranged your life together this way?
    *   Does it seem fair to each of you?
    *   Are there some things you would like to change?
    *   How can you work together to make these changes possible so that your partnership will be even better?

Is equal pay for equal work a male/female issue? Is it cultural? Is it race-related?

The roles a couple chooses, or consciously doesn't choose, may be influenced by parents, other family members, friends. Are there people in your life who make changing roles more difficult for you?

Sometimes an individual's employment can establish more power in a relationship than either individual. Time demands may include on-the-job hours beyond the typical eight-to-five day, extended travel requirements or on-call jobs that have first priority over other partner roles. How does this overriding circumstance impact the couple relationship? Is it a negative or a positive impact?

Tips for Strengthening Your Relationship

1. Marriage is a team effort. Your job is to work together to increase each other's happiness.
2. As a couple, build on the important similarities you share, rather than the differences.
3. It's not about the structure of the family—it's about the function, and how people love and care for each other.
4. We are all different and unique. See your differences as a couple as strengths, not as problems. Partners each bring important gifts to the partnership.
5. Remember that important principles of communication are listening carefully and respect for each other.
6. An unequal share of the workload, even if viewed that way by only one partner in a couple, can jeopardize the partnership. Communication and fairness are key concerns. Be willing to discuss unhappiness in the division of labor; and be willing to negotiate changes if the workload is viewed as unfair by your partner before resentments overpower the relationship.

CHAPTER 9

Values, Beliefs, Behaviors, And Cultural Differences: Can We Love Each Other When We Aren't Precisely the Same?

The short answer to this long question is, "Certainly."

The longer answer is, "To do this successfully, you've got to learn to really listen to each other, respect each other, and spend a lot of time talking from the heart about who each of you is and how your backgrounds and views of the world are different. And this is okay."

Why Are People so Uncomfortable with Differences?

This is probably an impossible question to answer but a fun one to talk about. One interesting thread of discussion goes back through countless millennia to the origins of human beings. Ages ago, when most of the people living on earth spent their time traveling from place to place to hunt and gather food, small groups would occasionally encounter each other. Sometimes these encounters were friendly and sometimes, because of competitive pressure for food and other resources, the encounters were not friendly. As the theory goes, different groups began to identify themselves by creating markings on their skin, different articles of clothing and adornment.

People in different tribes quickly learned to identify those groups that were friendly to them and those that were hostile. An individual's ability to quickly identify the difference between a red feather adorning a stranger's hair and a blue feather could easily mean the difference between living and dying.

Parents passed these survival tips about human differences down from one generation to the next; thousands and thousands of years later we still pass such information from generation to generation. The problem is that we sometimes pass down the wrong information: prejudice and hatred. Individuals aren't born to mistrust and dislike people from other groups. Babies aren't born with hatred inside them.

As a member of our particular group, we live by social rules that have been developed over time. These rules were put in place to strengthen the group and help the members develop closer bonds. Within the group or couple, one individual may take the role of enforcing rules more literally than others. These negative views and biases insiders have about outsiders need to be *unlearned* if we are going to get along well with the many diverse members of our larger communities and build positive relationships outside our particular group.

And, couple relationships being what they are today, we are increasingly mixing and matching up as partners come from very different ethnic and cultural groups. Feelings of attraction and love toward our partner help us transcend what we may have been taught about color and culture. We are increasingly finding ourselves attracted to *outsiders*—people outside our so-called tribe. To build a strong relationship with this outsider we are in love with may take some extra care, caution and consideration.

Values and Beliefs = Expectations

All human groups, including families and couples, need values and beliefs to guide them. Values and beliefs that have been learned from childhood seem hard-wired into us as adults. They form the basis of our expectations. When you are a child and say to another child, "That's not how we do it at our house!" it's just an observation of a different way of thinking or doing. When you are in a couple relationship and one person says, "Why do you do *that*?" it may be heard by the partner in a different way as, "That's not how we did it at our house!" which although factual, may feel like an attack and a failure to meet the expectations of the partner.

When picking a partner it is wise to pick a person who is basically compatible with the broad belief system you embrace. But don't ever expect a perfect fit because we are all unique individuals and there are infinite ways to look at the world.

Be satisfied with agreement on the general principles of the good life. To demand in great detail what our partner should believe is looking for trouble. Of course, for couples and families to function well, they have to be in general agreement on basic principles of successful living. These principles are likely to include age-old beliefs that are endorsed by all the great and enduring religions and philosophical models for humankind: love one another; treat each other with kindness; find meaning and purpose in life by dedicating oneself to the greater good; believe that you are not the center of the universe but only a drop of water in the ocean of life, and so forth.

Fighting over the details is a recipe for trouble in a relationship.

Prioritizing Values

A value is something you hold as important. Consider the following checklist of couple values and *individually* number from 1-15 in priority order the things you each value the most.

Once you have each developed your list, discuss together why each set of values is important and how you can work together to strengthen your support of each other's values.

- Nature
- Time alone
- Spirituality
- Social events
- Money
- Prestige
- Power
- Health
- Appearance
- Education
- Home ownership
- Sharing household tasks
- Sexuality
- Time together
- Talking about issues

113

Looking at Differences with Confidence

It is especially important for a couple to talk through their differences and be united, for the couple will sooner or later face the extended family—the mothers and fathers and brothers and sisters on both sides of the kinship network. The extended family is likely to focus on differences rather than similarities and the discussions will begin all over again. If the couple has done their homework and carefully thought through their similarities and differences, they can face the rest of the family with confidence and hold their own while supporting each other in the discussions. When presenting your decisions to your parents, state your choices in terms of *We*, rather than *his* decision or *her* decision. This demonstrates that you are united on the decision.

Older generations grew up in a very different world than the world young people are living in today. Older generations in the family may bring a different mindset and see the problems that can be linked to differences rather than the strengths of the relationship:

> She can't marry a [Pick one: white man, black man, Asian American, American Indian, Hispanic . . .]. He just won't fit in the family and what will the neighbors say?!

—◆—

> Why can't she fall in love with a man? What is she thinking, falling in love with a woman? This is going to bring nothing but trouble for her and for us.

—◆—

> A Muslim? What could he possibly see in her? What's wrong with the good Lutheran girl down the block? What's the fascination with someone from the other side of the ocean?

—◆—

She's in love with a Republican? We've been Greens for 20 years. What will we do at family dinners? We won't be able to talk politics anymore!

The extended family looks at the couple's relationship from the *outside in*, and is very likely to focus on color differences, religious differences, political differences, sexual orientation and so forth. The individuals, to become a couple, have transcended these differences to a considerable degree and do not see them as crucial difficulties in their relationship. The couple, looking from the *inside out*, has concluded that their strength as a couple is founded upon things more important to them: mutual respect, shared ethical values, trust, honesty, dependability, enjoyable time together, openness to change, friendship . . . a long list of intimate relationship qualities that bond them together.

If the partners can help extended family members see the newcomer from the inside out, the extended family may welcome the new person into the fold. If the couple has not worked together carefully and thought all these things through as a team, however, they may be split apart by the extended family's initial objections to the "outsider."

Reality and Rose-Colored Glasses

After the initial excitement phase when the romantic period of the relationship starts to cool a bit, the differences between the two individuals may look a bit bigger (or much bigger). This can be especially true as couples disclose and exhibit more of their personal beliefs, attitudes and behaviors. As they interact with each other regularly on a day-in and day-out basis, things about the partner that might not have surfaced or been acknowledged may become more obvious and unnerving. Things that seemed small in the early romantic phase of the relationship can start to grate as the months and years go by, and this is the point at which good communication and conflict resolution skills are essential. By listening to each other and agreeing from the very beginning that you don't have to see the world in precisely the same way—you don't have to be clones of each other—these differences can be dealt with positively. For example, one couple we know mixed the Jewish faith and the Protestant faith in their marriage:

115

The result has been wonderful. I am continually learning fascinating stories and customs from Judaism that go back thousands of years. And the kids like having more holidays and festivals to celebrate than their friends whose parents share only one faith.

Groups of human beings often try to control the behavior of their members by dictating what each individual should believe and find important and meaningful in life. The reason for this, supposedly, is to strengthen the group and make the members more closely tied together. Another reason that is hardly ever spoken, however, is that group leaders often simply enjoy having the power to control other people and find satisfaction in making others jump on command, including the command to believe everything the leader believes. Related to this, the leader may feel so insecure and unloved in life that he or she may be trying to gain love by demanding obedience. The problem is: Love is very different from obedience.

Dictatorial approaches may succeed for a while in getting someone to do what we want, but in the long run fail because they are motivated by fear. In a family or in a couple relationship one person might aspire to be a leader but if he or she becomes too bossy as a leader, the rest of the family or the partner eventually respond negatively by actively arguing against the overbearing individual or by living a lie, going behind the domineering person's back and doing what they please in secret. The feelings of closeness and connection between people are nurtured by caring, love and kindness toward each other.

Another useful value to hold is the belief that differences can, in themselves, be a source of strength. In American government, for example, the political party system is strong and lively. When politics become so divisive that the system comes to a halt because the parties cannot agree on anything, many Americans get fed up with politics and turn the television off. But to have no open and spirited discussion of important issues could be a major problem in our society. Since the answer often isn't all that clear—one side has a bit of the truth and the other side has a bit of the truth—a workable solution to a particular problem is likely to lie somewhere in between.

Love flourishes in an atmosphere where people are free to be who they are and believe what they wish to believe. If one of the partners aspires to leadership in the relationship, the kind of leadership that is most helpful and productive is *servant leadership*. Servant leaders don't try to dictate to their partner and other members of the family. Instead, they dedicate themselves to helping their loved ones grow, learn, and become happier, more engaged and fulfilled in life.

The Big Issues: Religion, Politics, Sex, On and on . . .

Can a Christian love a Buddhist?

Can a Muslim love a Hindu?

Can a Republican love a Democrat?

Can a man love a woman?

Taken altogether these seem like an odd collection of questions, don't they? But look closely and the meaning is clear: Many people around the world get wound up about religious differences and believe they cannot be resolved; similarly, many see political differences as hopelessly divisive.

And yet, gender differences seem *different*. Yes, a man can love a woman, and vice versa. It happens all the time and the key is that though the two *are* different, we have learned to enjoy and find satisfaction in the differences. We honor the differences, we love the differences, and these differences add spice, excitement and the topic for countless conversations that have gone on endlessly around the world.

So, why do religious differences, political differences, ethnic differences, cultural differences, racial differences and sexual orientation have to be such terrible hurdles for people?

The truth be told, they don't have to be big hurdles at all. Small hurdles, maybe. But not big. And, among many couples the differences are overshadowed by the similarities they see between each other. Going back to the red feather and the blue feather: When you think about it, all human tribes are much more similar than different, and to sustain peace in the world we need to focus more on similarities than differences.

Individuals from different religious or political or ethnic or cultural groups fall in love with each other every day. The couple finds that they enjoy each other's company, they love talking with each other, they find comfort being around their partner, they admire their partner's honesty and generosity, they find that they work well together, that their partner excites them sexually, and so forth. These relationship strengths loom large

117

in their feelings toward each other, and the differences seem smaller and smaller as the perceived strengths grow.

Similarly, two heads are better than one in a couple relationship. One partner's view is no doubt going to be somewhat different from the other partner's view, and by *putting their heads together,* they come up with a better solution than by simply going it alone.

The important ground rule we have noted before still applies here: During these discussions over differences the couple has to keep telling themselves that they are on the same team. They are not on opposing teams trying to beat each other, but on the same team working together to find a solution to a difficulty and thus, improve the quality of their relationship.

This is not easy to do, of course. But it is essential to keep trying!

Differences May Be Tied To Individual Temperament

Temperament or personality traits can be a significant factor in some relationships. Both partners may have very similar traits and closely share values, beliefs and behaviors. Other couples may be polar opposites. Most times these temperament choices are either comforting or exciting. When we have little issues to discuss, temperament—coupled with how we learned to handle differences—can make the situation like the dead of winter or the 4th of July!

The partner who is very organized and detail-oriented may want things discussed immediately and may have high expectations as to how the discussion will take place, as well as a good idea of how the discussion will end! A laid-back, very flexible partner may never see the need to discuss these differences. This person may have a *laissez faire* attitude: "Yeah, we think different things. So what? That's natural." Some people are very sensitive, caring, peacemaker-type individuals who are ready to adjust to any situation for the sake of their partner and the relationship, even if they really aren't in agreement with the adjustment they are making. There are occasions, however, when too much satisfying the other half of the partnership may cause resentment in the peacemaker, and what once seemed like an agreement suddenly becomes a huge disagreement. Another individual might have a temperament that is very self-contained and inquisitive, guarding thoughts to a greater degree than most. A *thinker* like this can cause confusion in a relationship by the constant evaluation of any given issue, which results in conclusions that change repeatedly over time.

Although no person will only have qualities of one of these temperament styles, some individuals will display much stronger examples than others. No temperament or personality type is *wrong* and no temperament is more *right* than any of the others. The importance of realizing temperament differences is that it is one more tool for couples to use when coming to a greater understanding of each other and how they can make the best of each other's differences. It's important to realize that we aren't all going to think alike and it's okay *not* to think like everyone else! Different ways of thinking are reflected in the way we act toward each other in life. One wife, after learning about personality differences, exclaimed: "My husband really does love me! He just shows love a different way! He shows he loves me by making sure my car is serviced and filled with gas." Once she realized how her husband thought, she realized he did care about her but just in a different way than she defined caring.

The Little Issues: These Can Be Big Ones, Too

Compromise and negotiation are important when discussing the big issues in which people differ in relationships, but often couples overlook the trivial things. Little issues that happen over time seem to build like layers on an onion. No single little issue is that important, and one can excuse an occasional irritation. But when those small issues continually go unaddressed, negative attitudes can develop, irritations fester and confrontation can be the ultimate conclusion to *just one more thing*. The point here is that the onion layers need to be peeled back one by one, as they build. Don't wait until the onion is complete. Approach discussion on each item as it becomes an obvious concern to one partner. Look at it as a layer on the onion that needs to be removed, rather than allowing it to build up.

So what are some of these so-called *little issues* we refer to? One that most couples deal with at some time in their relationship is how to handle holidays important to both extended families. There are traditions and expectations to consider, as well as finding time for everyone to get together without causing distress for the couple or the extended family. Like it or not, there are times when a couple has to admit that the extended family really is part of the equation of the individual. Little traditions influenced by family, community and childhood rituals are imbedded in each of us. And they aren't always going to be complementary to the traditions that are important to our partner. Another less complex issue is the proverbial *toilet seat up or down* discussion. But you get the picture: Little things can become Big Things if we don't have the courage to discuss them when we are thinking rationally.

Even though we fall back on our childhood imprints of behaviors and traditions, they may not be what we truly want to follow. As a child did you ever think, *I'll never say that*, or *I'll never do that to my kids*, but now you find you do those very things or behave that same way your parents did? Our growing-up influences are great and can be enduring, whether they are positive or negative influences.

So, how long does it take to work through all the little issues? You never do! They must be a constant source of attention down through the months and years, for they come up all the time. Your relationship becomes what you focus on. Make a habit of positive thinking. If you focus on the negatives—the little issues—that is all you will see. The opposite is also true. If you focus on the positive, you will find more positives in your relationship. When you think about the positive side, the negative falls away. Don't look at this process as a problem, however; instead, reframe it as a sign of ongoing growth in the couple relationship—another chance to strengthen your love for each other by understanding your partner better.

Little Issues	*Strengths to Share*
We all have *little issues* we can identify. Here are a few common little issues to get you thinking. Add to, cut or change this list to reflect the items on your personal *Couple Little Issues* list in a more positive way.	Now think about the things you *really appreciate* about your partner. These may be traits or characteristics you are very aware of. Or, you may realize there are several traits you haven't acknowledged, but to you, these are very special characteristics about your partner. Make a list of these special traits. Here are a few ideas to get you started:

Little Issues:

- He tracks mud on the carpet and doesn't clean it up.
- She leaves laundry hanging in the shower.
- She parks her car over the line in the garage.
- He will never empty the dishwasher.
- He never dresses up when going out for the evening.
- She is always late.

Once your list is created, it is important to discuss your entries.

- Why do you feel this way about each issue?
- Where did you learn to make this an important issue?
- Is this an issue the two of you can be more flexible on?
- How can it be changed, or does it really need to be changed?

Strengths to Share:

- He always asks how my day went.
- She takes time to talk at night even if she has other tasks planned.
- He always empties the trash.
- She always looks beautiful.
- He never leaves the house until he kisses me good-bye.
- She is great with the kids.
- He always pays the bills on time.
- She's willing to go to ball games with me.

Each of you take your appreciation list and in a quiet, relaxed environment, share your thoughts about each item with your partner. When you are the message recipient, don't object to the compliments, savor them. When you are the speaker, enjoy the gift you are giving.

Differences Can Be a Source of Strength For Couples and Families

Throughout its history, America aspired to be a melting pot, a place where people from around the world immigrated and blended together to become one united people. This has happened to some degree, especially for those in the white majority. But for those who look different, the task has been much more challenging and the barriers to full acceptance remain high.

In earlier days it might have been possible for some Americans to isolate themselves from other groups of people, but with the changing demographic landscape of this country, hiding away from each other is impossible. Today as the cultural makeup of the country continues to change, it is predicted that in the not-too-distant future people in the various minority groups will outnumber those in the majority. Within a few decades the total number of African Americans, Asian Americans, Latino Americans, Native Americans and other minority groups will be greater than the number of European Americans.

People are continuously immigrating from country to country the world over. As long as there are new immigrants into a particular country, the country probably never will become a true melting pot because the process of changing one's cultural orientation generally takes two or three generations or more. Since America more than two centuries after becoming a country has not yet become a melting pot and is not likely to do so in the near future, many observers have argued for a different vision for our country as a whole and for its people.

One metaphor that resonates well is that of the *symphony*. If our country were to become in some ways like a symphony, we would each retain our unique characteristics as individuals—like the many different and unique instruments that play in a symphony orchestra—but we would also learn how to work together as a team and play beautiful music together. Rather than all meld into one gelatinous glob, we could instead preserve diverse cultural characteristics while pulling together effectively when the need arises. Couples can create a new symphony in their family by celebrating special traditions from their families of origin and creating new traditions important to their new nuclear family.

This may all sound hopelessly idealistic and the chance of a whole country swimming in the same direction for very long is unlikely. However, on the more manageable level of couple and family relationships, there are countless smaller symphonies playing happily together. Think of your family and the families of your friends: What kind of ethnic and cultural mix do they have? Is there a mix between farm and city? Private education and public? Blue collar and white collar? Chances are there is a good deal of diversity in the micro-world of your own family. And if things are going well in these families with diverse members, odds are that the family members are not spending much time thinking about how *different* everyone is, but instead, are focusing on the family members' *strengths and similarities.*

Very Short Stories from Real People

> My son, who is married and living with his wife and family hundreds of miles away, just wrote me a long letter explaining why he doesn't believe in God. Now, I'm a devout Christian but when I was young I also had my own doubts about religion and did a lot of thinking before I settled on my own belief system. I enjoy talking with my son about his beliefs and I'm proud that he feels comfortable talking with me. I don't get mad at him for not believing what I believe, because I don't want to drive him away. I want to share with him what religion has given to me and hope he finds beliefs that bring meaning to his life.

> I can let the dishes drain on a tea towel on the counter if I'm in a hurry. My beliefs are that you NEVER leave dirty dishes in the sink or on the counter, but clean dishes are okay. My husband can't move forward until the dishes are dried and put away, even at the risk of being late. He says, "My Aunt Martha [who raised him during a chaotic and impressionable time in his life] would never do that!" So whose right is right?

People ask me why I am a lesbian. I've thought and thought and thought about this for a long time and the best answer I can give to the question is, "Because I had such a warm, loving and accepting mother and father. Many of my friends who are gay have been rejected by their family, disowned and thrown out. I have been very lucky to have such thoughtful parents who listened to me, talked with me, and basically said they would love me no matter who I love. They don't really completely understand me yet—who really can understand another human being?—but they have decided that they want to keep caring for their daughter rather than losing her or throwing her away.

Can a Democrat love a Republican? Stan and I continue to love each other now for more than 30 years, yet we are so very different in so many ways. But deep down I love him for the good and kind and honorable man he is, and he loves me for the good qualities he sees in me. Being a Democrat or a Republican is a small matter, when you really get down to it.

Years ago as my husband and I were on our honeymoon in Estes Park, we went to the grocery store to buy supplies for our stay. When we hit the peanut butter aisle, the brand came into question. We each held fast to our brand of choice; neither of us budged. Our tempers rose, our mothers' reputations were called into question and, in the end, no one felt like eating. We were left licking our wounds.

Discussion Questions

1. Think about your own extended family from a cultural perspective. What different kinds of cultures are represented in

your family? Have these differences brought some surprises to you and broadened your view of the world?

2. What are differences that have occurred between you and your partner that you did not anticipate? Tell about a difference that you have happily resolved. Tell about a difference that you are still working on.

3. Have you ever been caught in the middle on an issue between two people you love? For example, a parent and a spouse. How did you deal with that?

4. Many communities in North America are changing today because of new immigrants. How has this impacted your family? What adjustments has your family made? How have new people to your community enhanced your family's life today? In what ways have you reached out to the newcomers?

5. How can your differences as a couple be a source of strength? Think creatively.

Tips for Strengthening Your Relationship

1. Even though we may each see things differently, together as a couple and a family we can be a symphony, all complementing each other's individual characteristics.

2. We need values and beliefs. We can share what we believe with each other but we have no right to force these beliefs on other people. And we cannot expect or assume that a partner's values or beliefs will change after marriage or over time.

3. Open communication is the key to discussing differences. Anything mentionable is manageable.

4. Differences between two people are acceptable and can even build strength in the relationship.

CHAPTER 10

Money Money Money:
The Best Things in Life Are Not Things

Money and Marital Happiness

Money can be a source of conflict in any relationship. Talking about debt while trying to win someone's heart just isn't very romantic. But couples need to learn to talk about money issues, because finances are the most common stressors for couples and families in every stage of the family life cycle, according to Jonathan Rich.

People have differing views on the importance of money. Some expect money to be saved for needs that may be years away. Others spend it more freely, with little concern for the future. Why is this? There may be several answers to that question. As in other relationship behaviors, we tend to follow the behaviors modeled for us as children. Parents who valued saving are likely to have children who have grown up to be *savers* as well.

Personality traits also may enter into opinions regarding money. Using *Real Colors*, a very simple personality inventory developed by the National Curriculum and Training Institute, people can be divided into four different temperament styles. When an individual is asked, "What do you use money for?" the answers are consistent with their temperament:

1. Money is for the necessities in life first, and the remainder is saved for a college fund, an emergency, for retirement or another important goal.
2. Money is used to make others happy by sharing or giving gifts, especially at unexpected times.
3. Money is for the basics. To a person of this temperament, it's almost a nonessential.

4. A steady stream of money is needed for entertainment, to try new things, to take advantage of social opportunities. Saving is *not* a focus for this type of person!

Past life experiences, modeling financial behaviors of one's parents and personality factors all influence the attitudes an individual will have about spending and saving money. Since finances are the source of conflict in so many marriages, it is essential that couples take time to get to know each other's financial background and values.

> My husband and I struggle with deciding how to manage our money. I am a saver; each month I want something going into savings. I also have to have the credit card paid off every month. My husband feels that a vacation is important every year. This is family time, he says. If you don't ever spend any money to have fun, the kids are gone or someone dies and the family has never had a trip together. Those memories are lost! He has a point. But if we are under stress trying to pay the bills, that affects our family, too! What would you do in this situation?

A significant amount of research indicates there is a strong relationship between marital happiness and finances. A study by David H. Olson, Amy Olson-Sigg and Peter Larson shows that happy couples are in agreement regarding how to spend money: They have similar beliefs about savings, debt and the use of credit cards. By discussing these issues and coming to an agreement, the couple can improve their relationship. Couples tend to be happier with the relationship when they discuss their individual financial philosophies and find they can agree on the important topics related to how they use their money.

Money management is an important aspect of a couple's commitment to be together. Strong families and couples will use the strengths they have developed *together* to reason through the financial issues they may encounter. Positive communication and commitment are both key factors that lead to financial success as a couple.

Having little or no debt, or a workable plan to pay off debt, was also an indicator of happy couples, according to Olson and his colleagues. Finally, trying to live within their means was a characteristic many happy couples shared. Even though many marriages have financial challenges, they work the problems out and come up with solutions that are comfortable for both. Communication, the ability to manage conflict and agreeing on money choices helps make a partnership strong and keeps the partners happy.

But for some individuals, money is a taboo topic. When couples don't talk about how money is important to each of them, saving for the unexpected and meeting financial goals in the future is not likely to happen. Financial practices within the family can cause conflict, especially if one partner feels the other has more control over the family's money. It is very clear: Positive communication about money and finding ways to resolve conflicts over finances are critical to a couple's financial success and personal happiness.

Learning how to communicate on tough issues such as money management takes a great deal of skill and patience. Find a calm, relaxed time to work through the issues; settle on ground rules to help maintain respect and openness; be honest and broadminded; find ways to understand each other's financial values to make shared decisions on the importance of spending in particular categories, such as donations, gifts, entertainment, and so forth. If you are really struggling, start with one simple area of your finances and work on it. When you are successful in that one area, find another area on which to agree. One partner trying to push the other partner along won't be successful. You've got to find a way to come to some agreement.

Joint Accounts? Separate Accounts? Both?

A new couple is full of joy because of all the things they will be sharing in life. Should a checking account be one of those things that are shared? It's not necessarily a given that new couples will merge their individual checking accounts into one joint account. Complications such as a previous marriage, child or spouse support, children belonging to one but not both of the partners, student loans, existing mortgages or credit card debt may mean that accounts stay separate. Sometimes combining both partners' income into a joint checking account can create confusion, add complications, cause resentment and power struggles as well as feeling a loss of autonomy and financial independence. Perhaps one person keeps his account balanced to the penny, while the other rounds her account up or down to the nearest dollar—or doesn't balance the checkbook at all!

Part of the discussion on how a couple may choose to manage the checking account may center around the *why* of each person's choice. Does sharing an account feel risky to one partner? Does not sharing an account cause a partner to become defensive? Emotional issues need to be discussed as well as the logistics of the type of checking account a couple will create.

One option is for each to put all earnings into one joint checking account. A discussion needs to occur in regard to who will have the checkbook, and maybe more importantly, who will have the account record with debit cards being the norm. Also, how reconciliation of accounts will take place and who is responsible for paying bills will need to be determined. And, it will be especially important to communicate about purchases to avoid overspending when two are using the same account. If one of the partners is deeply in debt or doesn't keep track of checks and ATM withdrawals, this may not be the best method for you.

Many couples today set up a joint checking account while at the same time managing their own separate checking accounts. Each pays an agreed-upon amount into the joint account, which is used to pay the household bills. And each person is allowed the freedom and some financial independence by having individual accounts for personal use. Money as power in the relationship is avoided with this approach.

Other couples choose to only have separate accounts and split the bills accordingly. In this type of arrangement, it is essential that couples be sure to set up their accounts so each can access the funds if one partner dies.

All things considered, choosing to have separate checking accounts or a joint checking account should be a mutually agreed upon decision that is satisfactory to both partners. Resentment over money can cause problems in a relationship if it is not addressed in a way that satisfies each partner. The best choice is one in which both parties feel satisfied with the way finances are handled and both feel they are being treated fairly. Partners have to honestly talk to one another about financial concerns as they arise. Postponing financial discussions will lead to tension and add stress. You don't want to let money be the cause of problems in a relationship.

My husband and I don't share a checking account. He likes to get down to the penny and I am happy if I am as close as $5.00. We decided long ago to have our names on each other's accounts, but not to fight about who spent what. I write some checks for household expenses, and he has others. We share decisions on purchases over $200 but we don't argue about the little things.

Common Financial Concerns

Couples and families often get caught up in controversies over *wants* and *needs*. The needs of a family are things the family members cannot live without. Food, clothing and a roof over their heads are good examples. The wants of a family are things that will make life more comfortable, make a person feel attractive or help an individual or family enjoy leisure time.

Couples and families should have a clear understanding of the difference between wants and needs. Once again, communication is the key.

It's easy for wants to become needs in the minds of individuals: "I need a new video game!" or "I need a new dress!" or "I need a new Lexus!" or "I need to go on a cruise for my honeymoon!" really translate to the less essential statement, "I want this stuff!"

The trouble is, people are often likely to want to spend a lot of money on wants and then end up with not enough money for genuine needs. When individuals practice being objective about what the wants are, and when a discussion takes place to help everyone understand the reasons behind the request, the family can make an informed decision and agree, even if reluctantly, to stay within the budget. Communication takes time and involves commitment from *all* of the members in the family if financial decisions are to be successful. It all has to start with the couple. If the two partners can figure out how to separate wants from needs, they then can teach their children to do the same.

Sometimes, when a family member overspends, a hard lesson is learned. The consequence of overspending may help the individual face the reality that the need for expensive clothes, or the need to have a new car, or the need to drink and gamble in Las Vegas means that there is not enough money left for the mortgage, and the poor choice impacts all the family members.

Creating a Spending Plan

Every couple may have different long- and short-term goals. Short-term goals are those that you plan to reach in less than a year. Long-term goals are those that generally take a year or longer to reach. This is a very important discussion couples *need* to have. Couples have to realize they may not agree on every goal, so each needs to compromise. To help couples stay on track with their goals, they need to write down their short- and long-term goals and review them often or at least once each year. When planning to make a big purchase, such as buying a car or home, the next step should be setting some financial goals.

One way to reach those goals and manage household finances is to create a budget, or spending plan. It helps determine how money is spent each month. It also helps the family to look at their needs, versus wants. The trick is identifying what is a need and what is a want. Each person will view this differently. Discussing what is spent each month is essential to maintaining the budget.

A monthly spending plan can keep a couple focused on putting needs first, and it also helps them plan so they can make room in the budget for a few wants.

Having a budget or spending plan is not always easy. You start out with everyone on board, but suddenly someone wants something that doesn't fit in the budget, or one person doesn't keep track of his everyday spending. Without good communication, the budget falls apart. A budget is a commitment. To make it work, everyone needs to communicate their needs and have a discussion about whether an item is truly a need or just a want. With communication and the budget, reality may tell the family that this is something that isn't affordable now, but may be attainable in the future.

Effective Record Keeping

Have you ever noticed that some people are better at imagining, dreaming or coming up with ideas, while others are better at working with numbers, facts and figures? When couples are deciding who is going to be in charge of paying the bills or balancing the checking account, it is important to know that some people are better at working with numbers and getting the bills organized and paid. Here are a few questions that you might ask when deciding who should be in charge of the bookkeeping. Which group of questions best fits you? Which example best fits your partner?

Example 1: Do you like to do puzzles, play strategy games or read books? Does your desk at work or home look orderly? Do you like to eat at the same time each day? Do you prefer to complete one job or activity before you begin the next one? When watching TV, do you watch the same shows? Do you always take the same route home each day? When you study or read do you like it quiet with no distractions?

Example 2: Do you like to be active, play sports, make a craft or draw or paint pictures? Does your desk at work or home usually have things piled instead of orderly? Do you usually like to eat when you get hungry, not at a set time? Do you like to work on more than one project at one time? When watching TV, do you switch channels to get the most interesting show on at that time? Do you take different routes home each day from work? When you study or read, do you turn on some background music, eat something, take frequent breaks and change position quite often?

If one of you fits *Example 1* very well, that person would likely make a good bookkeeper for your family. If both of you fit *Example 1*, you could work together and share the role of bookkeeper. Either way, it is important that both of you have a good, working understanding of budgeting and other financial matters so that you don't get in needless arguments.

The ability to be well-organized and work with numbers clearly isn't a skill everyone has, so talk it through with each other and decide if you both want to share the responsibility of keeping track of family finances, or if one partner wants to take the lead. Remember, though, that whoever keeps the books does not have the power to make all the financial decisions. Couples and families will be much happier with each other if they share in the power of financial management. If one person makes all the decisions, everyone else is likely to be quite angry on occasion.

Other considerations when deciding who will manage the family's books include experience, time and interest. For most couples, managing their finances means one person handles the day-to-day finances. Even though one person manages the money, trust and communication are still required. It is important to have the duties assigned so each person knows her or his responsibilities clearly. This helps to avoid arguments over finances, which, as we have seen, are among the most common arguments couples have.

Fitting in Savings

Money problems are often related to a couple's or a family's inability to develop specific spending and saving plans. It is important to get in the habit of saving from *Day 1*. One of the best reasons for saving is so that you will be prepared for a possible financial crisis like an accident, illness, pregnancy, job loss or divorce. Every couple and every family in their life together are very likely at some time to face a financial crisis.

To protect yourselves, at least six months of salary should be saved for emergencies. By following a few simple guidelines, couples can save 10% to 20% of their income per year. Thomas Garman and Raymond Forgue, experts in personal financial management, offer six guidelines for those who want to save money:

- Don't buy on impulse.
- Avoid buying on credit.
- Buy at the right time. (Avoid peak demand.)
- Don't pay extra for a brand name. (Look for generic items.)
- Recognize that convenience costs money.
- Question the need to go first-class. (Do you really need the best?)

To be able to meet your financial goals, you need to be able to save. The brilliant mathematician Albert Einstein is reported to have called compound interest "the greatest mathematical discovery of all time." By saving a few hundred dollars a month over 30 or 40 years, a person can become a millionaire. He called the formula for compound interest the Rule of 70. Take the number 70 and divide it by the interest rate. This tells you how many years it takes to double your money. For example, if you are making 10% return on your investments, divide 70 by 10 and you can see that your money will approximately double in only seven years. If you are making 5% return on your investments, your money will double in about 14 years. The beauty of compound interest and the Rule of 70 is the fact that your savings are growing, not only as you contribute new money to your accounts, but also because you are making interest on top of your interest. The interest you make also makes more money for you, as the interest is compounded. This is why your savings can double so quickly.

This formula works for you in the case of saving money. And it works against you in the case of borrowing money: Using the Rule of 70, if you are paying 10% interest on your bills, the cost of your purchase will double in only seven years. If you are paying 20% interest, the cost of your purchase will actually be double in only three-and-a-half years. For example, that stereo you purchased with your credit card will probably cost twice as much because of the extra interest you have to pay. The companies loaning you the money usually don't go to a great deal of effort to point this out to you.

In sum, you can win big when you are saving money, and you can lose big when you are borrowing money.

Children learn from the example the adult sets. One way to teach your children how to save from a young age is to give them three containers. One container is for spending money, one is for savings and one is for giving (for favorite charities, a religious institution or family gifts). The children can earn a monthly allowance and be responsible for certain chores. This teaches them to think about where their money is going, to be generous and to save for the future. Parents can be very instrumental in the financial education of their children. As one young man explained, "When I started working, my dad told me to put money in savings every month. He told me to try to save about 15% of my paycheck. Because I followed this advice, I was able to buy my car without having to finance it."

By helping children in the family learn how to save when they are young, they will be likely to carry this habit forward successfully into adulthood.

Purchasing a Home

Owning a home can be very important for a family in developing a sense of unity and togetherness, and the extra space is always welcome. Owning a house forces one to save. Generally speaking, in a reasonably good economy, each payment represents an asset that is growing in value. A homeowner can borrow in a pinch against equity as the value of the home increases. A percentage of the interest you pay on your home mortgage is also deductible when filing federal income taxes.

Monthly housing expenses should consume no more than one week's take-home pay, so it very important for couples to look at what they are earning to be sure they have enough to continue to make a monthly payment. As a general rule, buying a home is a better investment than renting. For couples that have a hard time saving, this is one way to save. And, if you are able to make an extra principal payment or more each month, you can significantly reduce the amount spent on interest and the years needed to pay off the debt. Look online for a mortgage calculator to see the difference it would make for you. One proud husband explained that by adding extra dollars to the house payment regularly, he and his wife were able to pay off the house completely in 19 years instead of 30: "That was sure nice to get that all done when we were still relatively young."

There are also disadvantages of buying a home. It is a big commitment of time and money. It can be an emotional drain. The cost of maintenance and repairs can be high. Couples get in trouble with the high cost of maintenance and repairs if they don't save in advance for upkeep. It is suggested that when a couple begins home ownership, they start a savings account for the house. A set amount should go into this savings account each month to help out when the furnace stops, the air conditioner goes out or other repairs are needed. Being short of money when house emergencies take place is one way couples get behind and debt starts piling up, leading to disagreements and arguments.

Credit: Friend or Foe?

Credit can be very convenient. It allows people to enjoy something while paying for it, buying something that is on sale and getting something needed when money isn't available. Credit cards can be invaluable when away from home and a crisis occurs. A credit card builds an individual's credit history. A positive credit history is needed to secure a loan when buying big-ticket items.

Some of the disadvantages of owning credit cards include the potential for high interest charges, very high late fees and increased interest rates if a payment is late. Credit cards have caused many families serious financial problems because they are so easy to use. When the monthly statement comes, if there is not enough money to pay off the balance and only the monthly minimum is paid, the amount owed starts to grow. When there's an unpaid balance, the cardholder starts paying high interest on that amount. Couples who continue to use credit and allow the unpaid balance to increase quickly find their credit habits are out of control. Making matters worse, many times couples will have multiple credit cards causing the debt to grow on all of the cards, not just one. The more debt you have as compared to your credit limit will result in a lower credit score. To prevent lowering your credit score, the recommended guideline is to use no more than one-third of your available credit.

Couples who don't agree on how to use credit cards find themselves in conflict. One person wants to pay off the debt but the other may not see how that is feasible. For that reason, as well as others, paying off credit card balances monthly is ideal. If this is not possible, the couple needs to discuss the quickest way to pay off the debt. One solution to help control credit card use might be to cut up your credit cards after your debts are paid. Remember, however, that cutting them up does not mean you have removed your name from the company's listings; you must follow up with a letter requesting that you be removed and that you will not be making any future purchases. Some couples who struggle with debt on their credit cards have chosen to keep only one credit card for emergencies when they are away from home.

Credit card debt can be a very serious problem for a couple. The ideal situation is to pay cash whenever possible and when there is a balance on your credit card to pay it off completely each month.

Sometimes a couple is overwhelmed with the amount of debt they have. Health problems and high medical bills, economic recession and job loss, drinking, drugs, and other addictive behaviors, and a long list of other financial difficulties can lead to a couple using a credit card for daily expenses, which is a bad situation in which to be. This is a short-term fix that can lead to long-term disaster. Credit cards have high interest rates and credit card debt is difficult to pay down. The amount owed compounds rapidly because of the high interest rate.

Countless couples and families get caught in the credit card trap. The best way to prevent this problem is to treat credit cards with extreme caution. Prevent future problems by knowing the difference between *wants* and *needs*.

Dealing with Debt and Bankruptcy

Here are some tips for tackling debt: If the number of bills seems overwhelming, find the bill with the least amount to repay and work hardest on that one until it's paid off. That sense of accomplishment will encourage a couple to keep on trying. Go for the second lowest bill next, and so forth. Meanwhile, don't forget to make the effort to pay minimum payments on *all* your bills; showing that you are trying will help keep the debt collector from knocking at your door. Work with the companies you owe. Make a phone contact to each business, explaining your situation and your plan for repayment. Don't just ignore the bill and hope it goes away! It won't.

Consider additional alternatives that may help bring in more money: Can some night work be added to your day job? Borrowing from family or friends can sometimes hurt relationships—keep this resource as your last effort and only ask if it is *absolutely* necessary. If you do borrow from those you are close to, remember you are indebted to them just as much as any other financial institution or business, which means they need to be paid back.

A couple is in essence bankrupt when they are in an extremely dire financial situation with many overwhelming bills to pay and minimal financial resources. In this situation, outside help is needed. A qualified professional 1) will know what alternatives can be considered; 2) is well versed in the requirements and expectations of bankruptcy court; and 3) can help the couple work through the options and determine what may be the best solution for their family's needs in the short term *and* the long haul.

Anyone considering bankruptcy needs to research the bankruptcy laws to be knowledgeable regarding what the repercussions are at the current time. Bankruptcy affects the life of a family for years after the filing has taken place; couples should be sure to know what those effects are.

The couple relationship can be impacted if bankruptcy *is* declared. Bankruptcy can lower self-esteem, cause partners to blame each other and weigh a person down with guilt. All of these are stressful and heighten conflict in the relationship. These problems can be minimized or overcome if the couple is prepared and knows what to expect. Once again, frequent communication that focuses on resolving the problem will make a significant difference.

Bankruptcy should always be seen as *the very last option* when dealing with financial problems.

Financial Education and Counseling

Excessive debt may be due to overspending, crisis spending, careless spending or other reasons. When there are many bills to pay, and not enough income, debt can get out of control quickly. After developing a plan, the couple can try it out for a few months. If the financial situation doesn't improve and money issues continue to be overwhelming, professional help may be an option.

Although professional help is often essential to gain control of your finances, the wrong person can add to already significant problems. Before hiring anyone, remember the *Rule of Three*. Always look at three people and compare them before doing anything. Develop a list of referrals through the help of family and friends. Gather information about the number of years the professional has been in practice and qualifications. Ask about fees and rates for services. Check references or names of clients you can call to ask about their level of satisfaction with the professional's services. Ask about any contracts that need to be signed.

Financial counselors or marital therapists may be able to help. If it is a problem of just working off debt, the financial counselor may be a good option. If, however, there are deeper marital or personal problems, a therapist might be the correct answer.

Avoid "credit clinics" when trying to work off debt. They can charge excessive fees for services. Some of these businesses advertise that they will negotiate new repayment schedules with creditors. However, you can work with creditors on your own or find nonprofit agencies to help you. Ask family members and friends, and look in the phone book or on the Internet to develop a list of people who might be able to help. Remember to ask questions first and learn as much as you can before hiring anyone.

Conclusion

Remember, individuals manage their economic resources in different ways, depending on their world view, life experience and family background. Just because you are in love does not mean that you think about money in the same way.

Learning how to work together successfully as a couple to manage your finances is not easy. But working together successfully is absolutely essential for your long-term financial stability and happiness as a couple.

Very Short Stories from Real People

We were really happy before we got married. We went dancing and skiing and just enjoyed each other's company a great deal. After we got married I think our differences kicked in. I grew up in a family that didn't have much money but we had a lot of fun and liked each other. She grew up in a family that liked each other and had lots and lots of money. It became very clear that I just wasn't making enough money to satisfy her needs, but I didn't think she would ever leave me. However, she did, after two years. She soon after married a doctor.

I like things. I mean, I like being surrounded by my stuff. Now, my wife doesn't like stuff. She calls it clutter. Given her own choice, I think she would live in one of those minimalist-type homes where it's all white and you have a couch and a rug and maybe one lamp. Not much else. She just doesn't like stuff. I like to tell her that without me she would live like a monk in a monastery, with nothing. Instead of buying stuff, she saves money. This is great, of course, but where does it end? We've got a new baby coming and we're both excited. But our house is so small—my wife doesn't want to spend money on a bigger house—the house is so small that I've got to get rid of some of my stuff to make room for the baby. I want a bigger house so I can have my stuff and we can both have our baby.

When the kids were growing up we didn't have an extra penny to spare. Now that the kids are gone and the house is paid for, we've got quite a bit of extra money laying around at the end of the month. What a change! So, I tell my wife to enjoy herself a bit. At Christmas I even gave her $1,000 in crisp new $20 bills. I told her to go on a spree. But here we are six months later and she finally spent some of the money just yesterday. She went to the thrift store and got herself some "new" used clothes. What can you do?

—◆—

She came to our marriage with no money and a lot of credit card debt. I came to the marriage with no debt and a chunk of money in savings. Now, it really wasn't her fault. Her family never had a penny and she scraped her way through college bit by bit. She worked 35 hours a week her senior year, but the debts finally caught up with her and she had to scramble. She was basically living off five credit cards and the debts finally got out of hand. Now that we're married, she's steadily trying to pay down the credit card debt, but it's going to take her five or six years at this rate. I have to give her credit: she's really good with money. Now, I could help pay off her debt and save her lots of interest money. But if I do this it would put the kibosh on my plans to save enough money to buy a neat new car. What should I do?

Discussion Questions

1. Do you share equally in making financial decisions?
2. Are financial decisions what you argue about most in your relationship? Why or why not?
3. Do you use a budget? Why or why not?
4. Do you have separate bank accounts or do you share one account? Which way do you think would work best for you as a couple?
5. How do you handle credit cards? If this a problem for you as a couple, what could improve the situation?
6. How are bookkeeping responsibilities shared in your household? Is it working out well, or should another option be considered?

Tips for Strengthening Your Relationship

1. Save yourselves a world of pain by talking about money before you get really serious.

2. A fair division of responsibility for expenses will usually be based on the amount of income of each partner, but other factors may need to be considered as well.

3. Family members should have a clear understanding of what *wants* and *needs* are for their particular family. To do this well, you need to listen intensely and respectfully and explain yourselves clearly and carefully.

4. A monthly spending plan can help keep a couple focused on putting needs first, and such a budget helps the partners also plan for wants.

5. The ability to organize and work with numbers isn't a skill that everyone has. Consider these traits when deciding who will be responsible for paying the bills.

6. Save money for an emergency fund first. Then save for wants. Either way, be sure to save money every month.

7. Helping children in the family learn to save when they are young is a skill that will benefit them throughout their lives.

8. Credit card debt should be taken very seriously. Ideally, it should be paid off every month without fail. Otherwise, you stumble down a slippery slope and soon are in above your head.

9. Bankruptcy should always be considered *the very last option* available for dealing with financial problems.

CHAPTER 11

And Then There Were Three
(or Four or More): Staying Connected
With Your Partner After the Advent
Of Children into the Family

It has been estimated that approximately 50% of all marriages today will end in divorce, and the majority of all divorces involve children. Our focus here is parenthood, and we will continue to take a positive, preventive, strengths-based approach. From our own personal experiences, we recognize the fact that parenting can be a stressful job. Parental responsibilities plus the countless other responsibilities couples face can sometimes stretch their relationship to the breaking point.

But we will also maintain here that *happiness is a choice* on which parents can build a strong bond as partners in one of life's great adventures: the opportunity to watch our children grow, dream and achieve, and experience the joy of passing our love down to the next generation.

This chapter will not be taking the much more common problem-and-solution orientation to parenthood. There are countless books and articles and Internet sites that focus on solving problems. Because we do not see parenthood as a *problem*, but rather as a *gift*, we will focus in this chapter on ways of thinking about our roles as parents, and we will develop some general principles or guidelines for couples to keep in mind as their family grows in size. Your attitude and the strengths of your couple relationship will make the difference between looking at parenthood as a hassle or a joy.

This approach is similar to the one we took in our earlier discussion of marriage. Rather than admonishing couples to *work hard at your marriage,* we chose to encourage couples to *find joy in each other and in your life together.* Similarly, children are not problems to be dealt with, nor are children pieces of clay to be molded into some image we might have for them. Rather, they are beautiful creations in and of themselves and the best way to be a parent is to look for the beauty in these little beings and enjoy growing with them as their lives unfold.

This is not to say that parenthood is easy, nor are we arguing that one should ignore the critical parental responsibilities for guiding, protecting and setting boundaries for the children. Parenting is hard work, but meaningful work in life is not a bad thing. There are many joys and accomplishments along the way. We are saying that a more balanced view of the parental role is needed, balancing responsibilities with the genuine fun of watching children grow and learn. Happiness is a choice human beings make in their life. And, happiness as a parent is also a choice.

Great Marriages and Parenthood

A team of university researchers, including John DeFrain and Nikki DeFrain at the University of Nebraska–Lincoln; LouAnn Woolman at Bellevue University in Omaha, Nebraska; and Linda Skogrand and Pam Morrill at Utah State University in Logan, is currently studying *great* marriages: not just *okay* marriages, or *satisfying* marriages, or *good* marriages. The researchers have chosen to raise the bar very high and look for couples who believe they have *great* marriages.

The researchers, to date, have collected more than 3,000 pages of written testimony from 85 couples who volunteered for the study and believe they have a great marriage. While poring through the written testimony, LouAnn Woolman found that many couples talked at length about *how children serve to deepen a couple's marital bond.* Most of the time in American society when we talk about parenthood, we focus on problems: How come my son isn't potty-trained? Why do my teenagers refuse to come home? When will my husband take more responsibility for caring for the kids? And so forth.

Woolman decided to focus her energy on the question of how parenthood can strengthen the marital relationship. We find this to be a breath of fresh air. Most studies of marriages tend to focus on parenting problems that can plague the marital relationship: how a focus on rearing the children takes away time and energy from the marriage. Very few studies explore the positive relationship between marriage and parenting.

The majority of studies on marital quality and parenting show a decline in marital satisfaction among couples as the years go by. Some researchers believe the decline begins not long after the honeymoon and continues throughout the marriage. Other researchers argue that marital satisfaction over time diminishes, then increases during the later years of the relationship. This has been called the U-shaped marriage gradient: The couple starts out as newlyweds on the top-left corner of the U. Their level of happiness with each other and satisfaction with their life is high in the early stages of the relationship. Things start to decline for the relationship with the birth of their first baby. Their happiness and satisfaction continue to decline until the children reach their teenage years when the couple reaches the bottom of the U-shaped trough. Job stress, parenting stress and other pressures all combine to lessen marital happiness and satisfaction during the teenage years.

Fortunately, for many couples it has been found that once the children start to reach young adulthood and empty out the nest, things tend to get better for the couple, now in their middle years. The stresses and strains of parenting teenagers and young adults lessens and the couple relationship starts to climb up the right side of the U-shaped gradient. By the time the couple has completely emptied the nest, things are looking good and tend to continue happily into the retirement years.

This down-and-up journey is the commonly told, traditional story of what happens to couples when kids arrive on the scene. In many ways, it is a sad story because it links a decline in marital quality with the advent of children into the family, and a subsequent rise in marital quality when the kids grow up and leave home. This story seems to make children a problem for couples rather than a gift.

We are happy to be able to say that there is a group of couples that managed to create a solid and satisfying life for each other throughout most of their marital life together: satisfaction with each other before children, satisfaction with each other while children are in the home, and satisfaction with each other after the children leave home. In general, researchers don't yet know how many couples manage to do this or what percentage of the general populous they represent.

But, when you listen to couples who define their marriages as *great, happy, satisfying* and *of high quality,* you hear what often turns out to be a genuinely heartwarming story. The U-shaped gradient in these stories is smoother: Marital happiness and satisfaction remain relatively stable through the marriage, from the newlywed days to the advent of children and on through the teenage years and the empty nest.

Yes, for these couples who believe they have great marriages (and often describe themselves as *best friends*), children were challenging on many occasions. But these couples found ways to keep their marital relationship strong and redefine parenting in a way that was not seen as a difficulty, but rather a blessing.

Don't get us wrong: We are not living in a hopelessly optimistic, Pollyannish world. We do not believe there is even one couple on earth that lives a perfect life together, that has wonderful children 100% of the time. We do not entertain that fantasy at all. We are realistic about life.

We *are* saying, however, that there are couples who have what can be honestly and realistically called *great marriages,* and these couples have reframed how they look at their job as parents and found ways to focus on the joy and meaning children bring to their lives as a couple. These couples have a great deal to teach everyone.

The Strengths of Great Marriages

As we studied what the couples in our great marriage research were saying, it became very clear that they view marriage from a strengths-based perspective. They portrayed their lives together as mixed with both joys and sorrows. They were not hopelessly optimistic, nor pessimistic, but generally realistic about marriage and family life together. But what is apparent about their descriptions of each other, their children and events in their lives is the strengths-based perspective from which they retell their stories. Whether recalling the joys of parenthood, successes in education and careers, or the sorrows over the death of a child, loss of health and separation during war, these couples recall shared memories as events that strengthened their marriage. These are couples that believe they have *great* marriages, not just good but of very high quality.

The International Couple and Family Strengths Model developed by John DeFrain, Nick Stinnett and many colleagues around the world includes six major qualities common in emotionally healthy marriages and families: appreciation and affection; positive communication; commitment; enjoyable time together; a sense of spiritual well-being and shared values; and the ability to effectively manage stress and crisis in the family. LouAnn Woolman created the following table, presenting the six strengths in the left-hand column and explaining each strength in the right-hand column using the words couples used to describe their relationship. The table is a very valuable resource, because it lists the strengths couples have as they describe for us what a great marriage is. In their own words the couples have clearly and simply described the elements of a highly satisfying partnership that lasts over a long time. And, these are the words of couples who have managed, for the most part, to enjoy both marriage and parenthood at the same time.

Marital Strength	In The Couples' Own Words
Appreciation and Affection	Love Hugs Kisses Glances Smiles Compliments Affectionate words and actions Courtesy Gratitude Security Romance Valuing each other Talking Caring Sharing Improving life together Sexual lovemaking
Positive Communication	Deep conversations about feelings and thoughts Sharing thoughts and feelings Regular conversations Taking enough time to communicate Respectful communication Active listening Anticipating each other's needs Positive nonverbal communication Calmness while communicating Delaying discussions until each of us is rational Saying sorry Being sorry Forgiving Walking away (but coming back later to resolve matters) Sleeping on it Resolving things immediately Compromise Accommodating each other Honesty A sense of humor Open-minded Tactful Positive Encouraging each other Non-blaming Resolve the issue and move on

Commitment	Persistent loyalty Giving of self
	Marriage as God's gift Our relationship as a priority
	The center of our life Trust
	Being flexible with each other Support
	Desire to age together Honoring our vows
	A lifelong promise Devotion to each other
	Emotional intimacy with each other
	My spouse is my priority
	Shared goals Honesty Faithful
	Dependable We will be there for our kids
Enjoyable Time Together	Enjoy activities together and with the kids
	Having fun together
	Simple things Friendship Love being together
	Not much separate time needed
Spiritual Well-Being and Shared Values	Share same religion
	Similar beliefs, ethics, and values
	Active in our beliefs Prayer
	Meditation Our beliefs are a core strength of our marriage
	Marriage embedded with divinity
	Loving God together
	Loving life and the world together
	Sharing our beliefs with our children
	Similar views on key social issues
	Providing good examples for our children
	Responsible citizens in our community
	Respecting each other's differences
	Respecting our marriage vows

The Ability to Manage Stress and Crisis Effectively	Exercise Vent Pray Meditate Support each other Block stress out Don't give up Positive attitude Face difficulties together Luck Planning Balanced lifestyle A cohesive family Healthy relationships Take one day at a time Prioritize Trusting each other Protect and help each other A sense of humor Laughter

See how you and your partner measure up today. Go back to the beginning of the table and, with your partner, talk about each item and circle it if you think it is a strength in your relationship.

What do you think? What are the key couple strengths that you have agreed upon?

Are there some strengths you would like to improve in your relationship?

Remember: These couple strengths are the basic foundation for a happy life together. And, fortunately, they don't cost you any money to improve upon. All you have to do is decide together that you are going to become strong in these areas, and then keep them in mind and work on them every day of the rest of your life! No one denies that being a parent is hard. But Woolman and her colleagues' study of great marriages and parenthood demonstrates that couples can be successful as parents and maintain close ties with their partners at the same time.

How Children Serve to Deepen A Couple's Marital Bond

How, then, do children serve to deepen a couple's marital bond? What are the couples who believe they have great marriages telling us? The research team, led by Woolman on this study, learned that children can deepen the marriage bond in many ways:

1. The parenting experience can improve the quality of marriage. Being parents does not have to diminish the quality of a couple's marriage.

2. Becoming parents can complete, unify or expand the marital relationship. Parenting can add greater meaning and depth to a marriage.

3. While none of the couples denied that parenting can be a challenge, many perceived these challenges as opportunities that drew them closer together as a couple.

4. Having children can help contribute many positive emotions to marriage: feelings of joy and happiness, laughter and playfulness are noted by couples.

5. Being a parent can help improve a couple's interpersonal communication skills and help them develop similar conflict resolution styles. This increases positive communication within their marriage, and helps them resolve disputes more effectively than they had prior to becoming parents. Parenting also gives couples more opportunities to communicate with each other.

6. Parenthood can help couples strengthen the sense of respect, fondness and admiration they have for each other, as they experience the parenting process together.

7. The birth of the first child can bring excitement, maturation and unification to the marital relationship. In terms of maturity, it has often been observed that parents raise children, but in another important sense, children raise parents. The experience of parenting can bring out the best in a person and a couple. The responsibility of guiding a child can mold a young adult parent in very positive ways.

8. A couple's experience as parents can help to strengthen their commitment to each other.

9. Parenthood can provide couples with a greater awareness and appreciation for the quality of their marriage.

10. Finally, the process of parenting can help to enhance a sense of "we-ness" to develop between the partners. Their parental experiences can become a team effort with a shared purpose and goals for their children. Being part of this parenting team traveling together on a great adventure can serve to strengthen the marital relationship.

One mother we know told her daughters that, "I am a better person because of you." What she meant was that the experience of being a parent had brought out her hidden potential as a human being in many ways. Raising children gave the young woman an opportunity to mature and learn how to focus on the needs of others rather than focusing so much on her own needs. Being a parent helped her develop patience, become a better problem solver, and become more creative in her thinking. And, because parenthood was helping the young woman to *grow up herself*, it helped her understand her husband and her relationship with him better. Fortunately, becoming a father had similar positive effects on her husband. In sum, parenthood had positive effects on their marriage.

Life Can Be Divided into Four Parts

The life of a couple with children can be divided into four parts:

1. *Life as a partner.* The time we spend with our mate.
2. *Life as a parent.* The time we spend caring for our children.
3. *Life as a person in the workplace.* The time we spend making money to support the family.
4. *Life as an individual.* The time we have just for ourselves. Time to think, to grow, to exercise and maintain our physical health; time to develop our spiritual side, and to be involved in our community.

A very common pattern that can be observed in our busy American society is for parents to succeed in two important aspects of their life—*Life as a parent* and *Life as a person in the workplace*—and to fail in two other important aspects of their life—*Life as a partner* and *Life as an individual.* It is very easy to fall into this trap.

This is how it happens: We cannot ignore our tasks as a parent, because our children need us to be connected, involved and responsible for them 24/7. So, we attend to our duties as parents very carefully. This is a challenging and intensive responsibility.

Similarly, we cannot ignore our responsibilities as an employed person in the workplace. We may tell ourselves that we can scale back the time we spend as parents by saying that we are focusing on "quality time." But if we tell our boss we won't be coming in to work much but we will give her or him "quality time," our boss is likely to laugh in our face. The workplace demands our attention and we will serve these demands because we know the consequences can be dire.

In a hard-driving society, parenting and work outside the home can easily be a more than full-time job. But, there are still two important aspects of our lives: our couple relationship and our personal health and well-being.

What commonly happens is that we care for our children and serve our boss, but because we are over-extended in life, we cut corners on our couple relationship and our personal health. We say to ourselves, "Well, I don't have any time to spend with [my wife] Sara this week, but she's a big girl and can take care of herself. Nothing can be done about it." What happens when we neglect our relationship with our partner over a long period of time is that our marital relationship erodes and the love we once felt turns to dust.

Simultaneously, we say to ourselves, "Well, I don't have any time for myself this week [to exercise, meditate, do fun things, pray, whatever it may be that replenishes us as an individual]. But that's okay, I'll get around to it when I can." What happens when we neglect our individual needs and spiritual health over a long period of time is that our physical health and mental health erode steadily and this is detrimental to our life as a partner, our life as a parent, and our life in the workplace.

All four parts of our lives are inextricably linked together, and when one link is weakened, our whole life is threatened.

In a very important sense, the couple relationship is the glue that holds our lives together. Our marriage in many ways is the foundation of our lives, and upon this foundation we build our lives as parents, as workers and as healthy individuals. Too often we let our life in the rat race destroy the relationship we have with our partner. And, as everyone knows, the winner of every rat race is still a rat.

If you decide that parenthood is stressful, if you decide that parenthood means only endless drudgery and conflict with your children, it will be so. Parenting can be stressful, but it is okay to be overwhelmed at times. Your partnership can help you overcome the difficult times.

On the other hand, if you decide that parenthood can be an exciting and fascinating adventure, you can be a parent who makes this happen. This is not to say that you (or anyone else, for that matter) control the world and can make everything in the world wonderful. But it is saying that *you do control to a considerable extent your attitude toward the world and your attitude toward your children.* Deciding to love your children and enjoy being with them is a major first step in making a grand adventure happen.

The story below told by a middle-aged man illustrates what we are trying to say quite well:

> My friend Jerry is a recovering alcoholic. He's been sober for more than 20 years and attributes a great deal of his success to Alcoholics Anonymous. One beautiful fall day Jerry and I were walking through the woods. I was complaining about my job and my wife and my broken-down car and the house that needed painting and my teenage kids and everything else I could throw into the mix. Jerry got a bit tired of my whining and said somewhat abruptly:
>
> "Joe, are you doing okay right now?"
>
> "Huh?" I replied.
>
> "Are you doing okay right now? Is life good right now?"
>
> "Well, yeah . . . it's a pretty day out. The leaves are golden and I'm enjoying walking with my old friend."
>
> "Okay," Jerry concluded. "Then focus on the beautiful day right now and don't waste your time and energy complaining about tomorrow and all the worries you have that might come true or might not come true. Enjoy *now!*"
>
> Jerry was right.

Focus on *now*, as Jerry suggests. Focus on the good you see in the world, the beauty you see in your partner, the joy you experience watching your children grow. Nurture your relationship with your partner, because that relationship is the foundation for your family. You can be the greatest employee and greatest parent and your life can still fall apart because you forgot to focus on the couple relationship, which is the glue holding the whole house of cards together.

Very Short Stories from Real People

Mom and I had always been pretty good friends. From the very beginning. Over the years she said many times how she didn't know much about boys when she got married. She grew up with a sister and didn't babysit much as a teenager in the late 1920s and early 1930s, so when I was born after World War II when Dad returned from the Army, it was quite an experience for her to raise a little boy. But, she rose to the occasion. She didn't see her job as a mother to mold me, or fix me, or set me going down the right path so much—the traditional view of childrearing. Instead, she simply enjoyed being around me as a young child: "You were always so interesting. Always so curious about things. I always enjoyed watching you grow and learn." Mom had the same attitude about little boys when my brother Jim was born almost six years later. She was, indeed, a magnificent mother.

I attribute one of my most important personality traits to her approach to mothering: I feel comfortable in the world, accepted, confident when I find myself in new situations with new people, because I was treated with kindness and respect from my mother early on. I have a foundation of self-esteem and self-confidence that she helped me construct as a young child.

The joy of being a parent also can lead to sad times for parents. The last few months have been very difficult for our family. We just got back from Ohio where we were visiting our oldest daughter and our new granddaughter. I must admit that as we drove home tears flowed for a long time as we realized that we wouldn't see our girls for months, maybe even a year. A few weeks later, we drove our middle daughter to college for the first time. Again, the painful experience of leaving her many miles away from home, though we were happy to see her growing up. And then, shortly after these experiences, we faced emergency surgery with our youngest daughter. Going through hard times with our kids, one right after the other, was almost more than we could take. Being a parent brings you great, happy times. And also times that are so very painful.

When we were young Mom and Dad would go everywhere holding hands. The grocery store, laundromat and church. They would sit in the porch swing on hot summer nights and sip lemonade and listen to the music of the crickets and katydids, while holding hands. They didn't say much, but they sent messages of love and respect to each other simply by holding hands.

After I married and had children, my husband asked what we could do to teach our kids about true love. As we walked along, I just smiled and held his hand tighter and said, "Oh, I think this is a good start!"

Discussion Questions

1. How would you describe your marriage: Okay? Satisfying? Good? Great? Explain why.
2. How did your relationship change when your children were born?
3. Do you see your children as a gift or a problem? Why? If you answered "problem," are there ways you can change your attitude?
4. What do you do to celebrate your marriage? Your children?
5. What have you done to meet the challenges of parenting?

6. Remember you are teaching your children about relationships every minute of every day. You are the role model. Do you like what you are teaching your children?
7. Share a couple examples of times in which your role as parent has strengthened your couple relationship.
8. When you divide your life as a couple into four parts (Partner, Parent, Workplace, Individual), do you feel your life is in balance? If not, what is out of balance? Share one way you plan to improve balance in your life.

Tips for Strengthening Your Relationship

1. Take time daily to talk together about anything BUT work, money, kids.
2. Recognize your mood and attitude can make or break your family time together.
3. Have a weekly date night. Better yet, have a couple dates a week and don't forget to talk with each other every day to keep connected.
4. Give each other a neck rub, foot rub, back rub. Positive touch raises the endorphins and your moods will lighten and your heart rates will slow.
5. Feed the relationship with honest exchanges of praise and thanks.
6. Enjoy every stage of your child's life. Remember parenting isn't a sprint—it's a marathon!
7. Present a united approach to parenting decisions. Discuss the issue together when you're alone with each other. Then present your decision to your child when you are in agreement.
8. Give each other a break in parenting. If one is having a difficult time with your child, recognize it and *hand off* the responsibility to the other parent for a time.
9. Support your partner when he or she is overwhelmed.

CHAPTER 12

Why Did We Get Married, Anyway?
What to Do When Passion Fades

For many couples, the early days, weeks and months of their relationship are a wonderful, warm-and-fuzzy fantasy world. What possibly could be more exciting than being in *Love Love Love*?

However, this state of perpetual excitement, powered by the high-octane fuels of *high expectations, inexperience* and *human biology* simply cannot last forever. The line between romance and foolishness can be a fine line, and the rude awakening comes all too soon for countless couples. The morning after just doesn't look as good as the night before.

Most every couple has a morning-after phase of their relationship, though at this point in the relationship the path diverges. For couples who can't seem to understand how naïveté and just pure lust cloud our vision and blur our powers of reasoning, the road toward a breakup is likely. These couples may conclude that they made a poor relationship choice and need to shop around some more for a better partner. Or, they may decide that they simply can't live without the thrill of romance and the joy of the hunt. So one or both partners may put out signals that they are once again available, even though they really aren't thinking about ending the relationship or a divorce. But when this happens—when someone starts feeling attracted to another man or woman and acts on it—the partnership that started with such high expectations is likely to spiral downward into disaster.

Other couples are more realistic and clear-headed in their thinking. For these couples, the path they have chosen leads them to a higher level, a new and more meaningful and sound relationship based on a rational view of the world and human beings, commitment, mutual respect and kindness, and in the long run, a regular dose of romance here and there for seasoning.

So, how does one decide whether he or she was fooled by romance and sexual excitement and should start looking again? And, how does one decide that the relationship is basically sound and simply needs some careful thought and effort? That, unfortunately, is something many learn through a bruising process of trial and error, in some cases many trials and many errors. Some people figure this out quicker than others, and their first marriage is a good fit that improves over time. Other people don't figure this out until their second marriage or third. Or never.

If you lean toward staying the course and holding on to your partner through thick and thin, many small things can be done every day to ensure success. Like gourmet cooking, the process of maintaining a healthy couple relationship down through the months and years is a both an art and a science. And, as we keep saying, it doesn't come easily for anyone but it sure can be a fun challenge, somewhat like a thousand-piece jigsaw puzzle but with an infinitely greater payoff.

For the process to work, however, both partners have to be committed to making the relationship successful.

"If Every Night of Your Life Were a Date Night, You'd Die in a Month"

Courting, dating, hanging out, hooking up . . . the terms people use for the process of finding a suitable partner change over time. But the basic dynamics never change. Or, at least, the dynamics aren't likely to change in the foreseeable future because human biological processes don't change quickly.

From a scientific perspective, natural processes have evolved through the millennia to ensure the survival of the myriad species in the living world. As the old song goes, "Birds do it, bees do it. . . ." And in human terms, sex drive is a powerful force for bringing two people together. Individuals caught up in this high-energy dance are focused, fascinated, excited, driven together by ancient biological mechanisms that they are not likely to understand.

Success from the perspective of natural processes means procreation. In the natural world, our sex drive rewards us with a baby and the beginning of a new generation of human beings. On the other hand, couples often are not likely to be thinking all that clearly about what success means from their own purely personal perspective. The forces bringing the two people together are not only rational forces—*We have similar values, We enjoy doing things together, She's got a great family, We both want children,* and so forth—but are irrational forces clouded by internal biological mechanisms that urge the procreative impulse down its seductive path.

The dating game, as it has been called, is a mesmerizing game for both players. It is a wonderful tidal wave of emotion to be caught up in. But frankly, if every night of your life were a date night, you and your partner would likely be at the point of physical and emotional collapse within a month. It's just too much for the body and spirit to manage over the long haul.

Fortunately, nature has found a way to save us from what could become overwhelming exhaustion. The seemingly inexhaustible and never-ending fires of passion finally do die down, thank goodness. This, however, is a difficult fact to grasp for many people, because passionate love can be addicting. When the throbbing heart settles into a more manageable rate, many partners make the transition fairly well while others are likely to miss the excitement.

The Grass Is Always Greener . . . Or Is It?

The desire to keep the excitement going, even though it's much more likely to settle into a calmer and more peaceful state, gets many of us into trouble. In a market-based society, we are constantly looking for a better deal. Comparison shopping is the norm. We scurry from store to store looking for the cheapest price we can pay for a particular item, or we look and look and look until we find the most absolutely perfect *Whatever-It-Is* that we think we need at the time. The skills we develop in shopping around and continually comparing things to find "the best deal" may make a little bit of sense when we are thinking about objects. But when we are trying to find and maintain a healthy relationship with another human being, our tendency toward constant material comparison can turn into the more dangerous game of constant social comparison.

Constantly comparing our partner with others in the social world is a dead end. It assumes that we can reduce human beings to bits and pieces that we desire; then search for the individual who has all the bits and pieces that we desire; and, thus, we will end up with the perfect model to fit our own needs. This type of approach may work when you're building a computer from scratch or buying a new car: "I need a two-terrabyte hard drive," or "I'll take the V6 with front-wheel drive, mint-green in color, preferably . . ."

But, this materialistic and self-centered approach to relationships ignores two important facts:

First, that each of us, as a total human being, is much more than the sum of our parts—we're more than the simple combination of an appealing body, and a great personality. The total person is much, much more than the countless pieces that can be found if we simply try to dissect each other in a biology class.

And second, this approach ignores the fact that our focus should not be so much on the characteristics of each individual, but on the characteristics of the relationship that these two individuals create together. Two perfectly molded individuals may have every individual characteristic that an ideal person should have: intelligence, good looks, solid family background, social competence, and so forth. But if they meet and simply don't dance well together, the relationship will not grow. There's got to be a bit of magic in the interchange, and magic is something generated between individuals; and it does not simply reside in one person or the other.

Grow is the key word here. People may come to a relationship when they are very young, hardly shaped and formed by life. People also may come to a relationship when they are much older, well formed and tested by their experiences over time. No matter at what point in their development they find each other, however, they will be forced to adapt to each other, to learn about each other, to see how they can fit together, and to find the will and courage to create a joyful partnership.

If the partners, instead, spend their time focusing on each other's weaknesses and problematic areas, trouble will brew. This approach assumes that the problems in the relationship are the fault of the other person, rather than thinking of the partnership as a team in which each individual has to work closely with the other to make the relationship succeed. And, if the individuals spend much of their time keeping an eye open for a better deal in the bubbling world of continuous social comparison, they will not invest the time and effort and good sense to create a loving relationship with each other.

An old adage warns us, the grass is always greener on the other side of the fence, suggesting that it is very human to believe there is something

159

better across the fence. Plagued by our tendency to make constant social comparisons between our partner and other men or women, we may come to believe we have made the wrong choice and just over the fence there is a *perfect* mate for us.

The trouble is, you might be dead wrong. You might be a victim of your own irrational desire for perfection that simply does not exist, and you might be a victim of your own need for passion that cannot be met in the real world.

For example, a friend from college called to share what had been happening in his life the last several months. It seems he had grown tired of his wife. He had focused on what was *wrong* with her and not on how the two of them, together, could build a strong relationship with each other.

He had found a sweet young thing at the office—*The grass was greener!*—and they quickly fell in love and fell in love with love. Soon after, he left his wife and she moved back to her home state to be with family and try to figure out what had happened to the marriage.

He stayed in the same city where he had met his new love. They had moved in together and were thinking about getting married. The fireworks subsided in a few months. The lust and heartthrob and all the other wonderful idiocy of *Love Love Love!* burned down and the embers were smoking but no flame endured. The new couple had settled into a routine, much like the routine that our friend had settled into with his first wife. The telephone conversation late in the night stumbled and paused and wandered to a closing and painful silence that lasted for perhaps 10 seconds but felt like an eternity . . .

"You know," the friend said, finally, his voice and his spirit sounding very, very small, "I think I blew it."

And he had. The marriage to the new woman lasted a few years and then they went their separate ways.

He had not understood that the search is not for the perfect partner. The grass is not always greener. He needed to know that the task at hand is to start out with a good partner, invest time, energy and love in the relationship, and for each individual to personally take the responsibility for helping the relationship to grow.

Being in Love with Love:
Emotional and Physical Affairs

We would propose that in marriage there is an inevitable process that can be called the Law of Marital Routinization. When you purchase a beautiful painting and put it on the wall in your living room, it jumps out at you, it captures your attention, you spend a great deal of time looking at it and enjoying it and loving the fact that you had the good sense to purchase it from the artist. But as the weeks and months go by, that beautiful painting that you love has become a routine part of your life. It continues to hang there on the wall, beautiful as it has always been, but you become used to it. It is always there, and sooner than you realize, it has become routinized in your world. When this happens, *Poof!* Your wonderful painting psychologically disappears from your view and you are off, chasing after other novel and, thus, more captivating things in life.

The Law of Marital Routinization that we propose here is that partners can too easily become like paintings: They quickly disappear from our radar as we zoom-zoom-zoom about, relentlessly focusing on other things that catch our eye. Novelty is the thing in our world today. It has to be *New* or it is not *Good*.

Now, here's the real story:

If you take *The Law of Marital Routinization* and add *The Grass Is Always Greener*, the witch's brew starts to bubble. Sprinkle in a dash of a very common and desperate fantasy, *Being in Love with Love*, and the danger of emotional and physical affairs outside the partnership escalates dramatically.

Please make no mistake about all this: being *Just Friends*, as many people like to kid themselves, is easily as dangerous to a marriage as a sexual relationship outside the marriage. The friendship drains energy from the marriage, and as the marriage becomes devitalized—lifeless— both partners become less interested in it and look for other ways to fill their emotional needs in life. And as they do this, the likelihood of leaving to join up with another partner increases dramatically.

In our society, people commonly believe that something goes wrong with a marriage and then one or both individuals in the marriage stray and find comfort in a new partner. Cause and effect: Poor marriage leads to an emotional and/or physical affair.

A more useful and realistic way to think about the cause and effects surrounding affairs is to say: Individuals seek the sparks in life they miss, so they look outside the marriage; as the affair grows in energy and passion, it relentlessly brings down what was basically a sound marriage that simply needed some attention.

Not all affairs are like this, of course. Some marriages are unworkable or destructive and cannot and probably should not be fixed. Marriages involving alcohol, other drugs, sexual abuse, and violence come to mind. But for many marriages that are faltering, the problems are not this severe and are in the realm of devitalization, which could be labeled the common cold of marriage. Every marriage gets devitalized every once and awhile, but it's not likely to kill you. Devitalization means that the couple's relationship has, predictably, lost some steam and simply needs loving attention.

The cure for the common cold? A bowl of warm soup. Some time in bed. A good sleep.

The cure for marital devitalization? Not much more complicated than the cure for the common cold. Loving attention and time together.

The danger is that when a marriage starts to become a bit devitalized, one or both partners will become attracted to outsiders. If this happens, they are likely to give all their loving energy to these outsiders, and this energy loss will topple the marriage. As we have seen, about 50% of all marriages are likely to end in divorce, and some counselors argue that extramarital affairs may be involved in 90% of these divorces. No one knows for sure, of course, because people who have affairs aren't very likely to tell the truth—either to their spouse or to a researcher studying the causes of divorce.

People have affairs with other people. They also have affairs with their work, with their children, with their church, with countless other things that they invest emotional energy in.

Think about it: If both partners forget to invest time, energy and creativity into their relationship and wander off into other things, who is to blame? If he has an affair with his job, working all the time, saying he is doing it all for his family when it's really about his own ego, who is at fault when she finds a boyfriend? And if she smothers herself in the children's activities to the point that she has left no space in her world for her husband, who is to blame when he finds a friend at the office to confide in?

The blame game quickly turns into a vicious circle and couples can get so caught up in anger and hurt and the urge for revenge that nothing good is likely to come of it all. Rather than framing the discussion around the question of who is to blame, it is much better to think back to the time in the relationship when things were going well. The focus should be on the time when the partners were attentive to each other and found comfort in each other's arms. Focus on bringing back the love you once had for each other, rather than figuring out who is to blame for the fact that it has disappeared for a while. Many marital and family therapists know that an extramarital affair can signal the end of a marriage, but it can also be a catalyst for growth in the marriage and a new, loving beginning for the couple. The choice is theirs to make.

But, before the inevitable *Law of Marital Routinization* grinds the partnership completely down, start finding countless little ways—every day—to keep the joy alive in a world that seems bent on wearing it down and burning it out.

The process of devitalization in a marriage is difficult to identify because it happens slowly and over time. The threads of the relationship slowly pull apart as the months and years pass, and the fabric of the marriage steadily weakens. One morning, one or both partners wake up and think to themselves, "I'm not sure I love this person anymore. Why did I get married, anyway?" When this has happened, it's an easy step to start looking for comfort from another man or woman.

Rather than fall into this easy trap, instead find ways to strengthen the marriage every day of your lives together.

A Great Marriage Is Like a Fine Wine: It Mellows with Age

Down through more than three decades of research on couple and family strengths, our research team has consistently found that marital relationships have the wonderful capacity to grow over time. Happy couples know this very well, of course, because they have seen how their partnership has become stronger over the years as they get to know each other better and better, and as they learn more about life and how to live it successfully.

In the early months and years, passion and the sexual bond the partners have with each other can sometimes carry them through tough times. They may not be very good at understanding and dealing with each other's differences yet, but a profound physical attraction for each other helps keep them together when their partner's quirks and thoughtless actions threaten the relationship.

Passion, as we have seen, inevitably cools down, but hopefully by the time that happens, the two have created a sound friendship on which to build their marriage.

So, when we recently advertised across the U.S., saying that we were looking for *great marriages* to study, we were not surprised by the response. Letters and emails came in from couples in 27 states, telling us about their marriage and why they thought so highly of it. And, the majority of volunteer couples were in their forties, fifties, sixties, and older. A smaller percentage of volunteers represented the thirty-something age group, and very few volunteers were in their twenties. We had seen this age-related pattern many times before in our studies of couple and family strengths, so were not taken aback in the slightest.

This result, weighted heavily toward older couples, could be interpreted a number of ways. One possibility is that the younger couples are just as likely to have a great marriage as older couples, but that younger couples are simply too busy to participate in a time-consuming research project. But, older couples are quite likely to tell you that they can be very busy in life, also, so we aren't convinced that *busy*-ness explains the research results.

We have concluded that the reason our sample of couples who perceived they had a great marriage was overrepresented by older couples was most likely because people really aren't in a good position to judge how strong and loving their relationship really is until they have been living together over a considerable period of time and met the countless major, modest and minor challenges life can present a married couple. In essence, you don't know how good a marriage is until you have been tested by fire. As one couple laughed, "You don't have any idea how good your marriage is until you have remodeled a bathroom together."

Or lost your job, had breast cancer, been flooded out, watched your baby son die, or personally witnessed any other of the countless tragedies that can befall a couple and family. We really have no idea how we will react as individuals and as a couple when very difficult times strike us. But we can be certain that, given the passage of enough time, the very difficult times will strike every couple and every family. We don't know when we will be tested, but we know the test, inevitably, will come.

Thus, older couples are in a better position to make judgments about their marriage, and older couples are more likely to conclude that, yes, they have a great marriage.

With all this in mind, we feel confident in saying that if a couple manages to stay together through thick and thin, the partnership is likely to improve with age. If the two can preserve their love for each other through the stress of life's inevitable ups and downs, their partnership is likely to become stronger and stronger. The relationship is in a solid position to mellow with age.

What precisely does this mean? That the rough edges are finally being sanded down. The bumps and bruises and misunderstandings and spats so common in the early months and years for many couples have largely disappeared as the two have grown more mature and understanding of each other's strengths and, shall we say here, weaknesses.

The couple has settled into a comfortable routine and routine makes life easier and happier for most of us, most of the time. We know what to expect from each other, and that can feel very, very good. The passion is still there on occasion, but not quite as overwhelming. Something better has replaced the passion: The partners are now *best friends*. They are companions in life.

There's Still Room for Some Sparkle

A comfortable routine, then, is good. Being best friends is wonderful.

But, as the *Law of Routinization* implies, too much routine is too much of a good thing. There's got to be some sparkle sprinkled in here and there if the marriage is to retain its luster and survive over time.

An old marriage counselor joke passed down through the years to today's marital therapists illustrates the problem very well:

There once was a woman who grew terribly distressed over the years because of her husband's inability to express love and appreciation for her. She felt she was good at letting him know how much he meant to her, but that he did not reciprocate the kind words. She finally managed after many discussions over many months to get him to go to a marriage counselor with her.

165

The counselor saw the root of the problem right away and said to the husband:

"Fred, please turn to Linda and tell her how much you care about her."

Fred furrowed his brow, fidgeted in his chair, grimaced, and finally blurted out to his wife:

"Dammit, Linda! When we got married 20 years ago I told you at the wedding that I loved you! If anything changes in the coming years, I'll be the first to let you know!"

That story captures a common difficulty of many people, especially men, the inability to express tender feelings. Sometimes in the dating phase of the relationship it is easier to express these feelings. Romantic emotions flood the brain and the kind words and thoughtful deeds pour out. But after the partner has been won over and the marriage has settled into its comfortable routine, the tender feelings and thoughtful deeds may diminish considerably.

The fact of the matter is that most of us want to feel loved and needed. This is an ongoing feeling that needs to be regularly nourished. Without regular attention, the warmth, the sparkle, the fire are likely to burn out and the couple is left with a devitalized relationship. And a lifeless marriage is a sad place in which to spend your days.

With a Little Thought and Careful Planning, You're Flying Once Again

So, when the partnership is at the point where the passion has inevitably faded a bit, where the sparks just aren't quite there like they were earlier in the marriage, what can be done to bring back some interest and a bit of the old flame?

Here are some tips:

S-L-O-W your lives down. Count up all the different things you're involved in and cut 35% of them out. They aren't as important as you think. You've just gotten yourself in the habit of running too fast and too long, and now you don't know how to slow the pace. If you can't cut 35%, cut 25% or 15%. The main thing: Cut the things that are not as important as your marriage. And if they are all more important than your marriage, you're in real trouble marriage-wise.

Spend more time together. Now that you've cut the nonsense and wasted motion out of your life, use some of this extra time to nurture your own personal spirit and the rest of this time to nurture your marriage. You loved being together when you were dating and you can love being together today.

Do something new and different together. It doesn't have to be expensive. Many happy couples have told us that their most memorable and meaningful times as a couple over the years have been when they were together, doing something new and different. Sometimes this meant traveling to a new place in the world. It doesn't have to be an expensive junket. You could go to a lake a few miles away from home that you've never visited. Or have lunch in a restaurant that just opened. The travel experience doesn't have to be elaborate or cost much money. And doing something new together can happen in your apartment or backyard just as easily as it can happen in Hawaii. The key here is that you are experiencing something new and interesting together. It's just a time for you and your loved one to enjoy life, hand-in-hand. One couple talked about how starting a new business together was a significant bonding experience for them.

Have at least one date a week. Better yet, two. Couples are never too old to quit having dates. It's a grand opportunity to stroll downtown together, chatting and window shopping. Or hike through the woods on the edge of the city. Go fishing, see a movie, go horseback riding, whatever . . . the main thing is that it's just the two of you. No kids, no cares, just like the early days of your partnership.

Spend time with other happy couples. Be sure to cultivate solid friendships with other loving couples. Getting together for potluck dinners is one excellent possibility. The main thing is having a chance, as couples, to share how your lives are going—both the ups and the downs. What happens is that you reinforce the importance of a happy marriage for each other. You find that every couple struggles in life on occasion, and that couples find ways to meet these challenges and continue loving each other. Limit time with negative couples.

Get away from the kids. Have some alone time. The best thing a couple can do for their children is to love each other and nurture the marriage day-by-day. The kids will quickly learn that you are not abandoning them if you spend some time alone together. They will learn, instead, that you love each other and love to be together and just focus on each other for a while each week. You can't afford a babysitter, you say? Then form an informal babysitting cooperative: You take your friends' kids for three or four hours so they can nurture their marriage, and vice versa. No money is spent by anyone, and their kids get to play with your kids for a while.

Work together to do some good for the world. Live your values. Show your children that you know how to put your beliefs into action. Instead of focusing all the time on your own troubles, focus on making life better for other people who are probably in more difficulty than you are. And enjoy the satisfaction, together, of doing something for your community that is genuinely worthwhile. We tend to love people who share a common purpose with us.

Be active together. Join a dance club, a gym, a volleyball team, go walking regularly together. It's hard to be depressed or angry with each other when you're physically active. Again, you can figure out ways to get your blood flowing without spending money. As one husband admits, "It's awfully hard to be upset about work when I'm walking with her, we're watching the leaves fall on a golden afternoon, and talking about how big the kids are getting."

Throw your TV away. It's a Pandora's box of sexual innuendo, violence and materialism. Or, if you aren't quite ready to do that, at least turn it off most of the time and invest your energy in talking with your partner and being physically active together. You'll be skinnier, less anxious from watching endless stories of how awful the world can be, less cynical about how hopeless televised political squabbles can get, and your marital communication will improve.

Make love. Start the long process of lovemaking when you get up every morning. Start by talking about life together, start by volunteering to run an errand for her, start by being interested in his day. Continue your lovemaking by eating dinner together, staying seated around the table and seeing how the day went. Continue your lovemaking by cleaning up after the meal together, washing dishes together, straightening up the living room, going for a walk, whatever. Finally, even think about continuing your lovemaking in bed as the evening wears on. If *tonight's the night!* make sure you begin this phase of your daily lovemaking early so you're not too tired. Why should we save this for the end of the day, anyway? Dessert could just as easily come first! And, instead of 5 or 10 minutes of this phase of lovemaking and drifting off to sleep, invest an hour: Start with a foot massage and an ankle massage and a calf massage . . . and a neck massage and an ear massage. You get the picture.

Making *true* love is not sex. It's much, much more. It starts long before bedtime, early in the day as you talk together, listen to each other, attend to each other's needs. And, this kind of making love is a strong indicator that there is a huge amount of life left in this wonderful, mature marriage that you are creating together.

Very Short Stories from Real People

> In our seventh year of marriage everything fell apart. I fell in love with a guy at work and after a few months of excitement and secret dates he took off after another lady and I learned what was really important in life. I stumbled back to Jason, shame-faced, and for some reason he took me back. We went to counseling and in this process we agreed that we both had forgotten to love each other. Instead we had focused on our jobs. Today we're doing great. We see that our marriage is the foundation of our life.

> I met an area farmer at a class on divorce that I was taking at the community college. As he described his plight it was obvious he was a workaholic . . . always working and never taking off time for his family. He had two young girls and rarely took the time to see them, much less take responsibility for their care. His first weekend with the four-year-old and five-year-old was challenging for him, so he tried to take them back early to their mother's house, but she would have none of it.

> As time passed, he was pleasantly surprised at how he had changed his priorities. His work was no longer the center of his world. He just had never put himself in his wife's place of holding down a full-time job and caring for the children. It was too late for the marriage, but he was really enjoying his daughters and the time they spent together. Hopefully,

he might respond to his next relationship by investing more in time and energy.

⎯⎯◆⎯⎯

When our daughter died we were beside ourselves with grief. She was only 11 years old and died in her sleep. For no reason. The doctors never found a reason. We felt terribly guilty, of course, and thought it was our fault even though it probably wasn't. We would sit on the living room couch all alone in the evenings and cry together, holding each other. It seemed to me like my wife was the only person in the world who really understood what I was feeling. And it seemed to her the same.

One evening Sherry looked at me and said, "You know, one good thing came from all this pain. Before Caitlin died we had been so focused on work and a thousand other things that we were neglecting each other. Caitlin has taught us how important we are to each other."

Sherry was absolutely correct.

Discussion Questions

1. What are the strengths of your relationship? Identify them.
2. Do you remember the characteristics that attracted you to your mate? Are these characteristics still significant to you now?
3. Identify the strengths of your partner. How do these strengths help support your relationship? Share these insights with your partner.
4. How do you express your affection to your partner? How can you learn to do this more often?
5. How much time, energy and creativity have you put into your relationship recently? What are some things you can do to increase this.
6. What are ways you strengthen your relationship every day of your life together?

7. List five things you enjoy doing as a couple. Use these examples for date nights.
8. Think of couples in your community that you admire. What couple strengths of theirs do you admire? How could you adopt these strengths into your partnership?

Make Your Own List of Tips
For Strengthening Your Relationship

What are your own best personal tips for keeping love alive in your relationship? As a couple working together, make a list and put it on the refrigerator. And be sure to follow this good advice!

CHAPTER 13

Through Thick and Thin:
Loving Each Other
When Hard Times Come

Let's talk about hard times. It can be argued that two of the biggest secrets of the 21st century are the fact that all couples face crises in their relationship and that a crisis can be a catalyst or cause of positive change and growth in the relationship. We don't tend to talk much about hard times in life, especially when our marriage is going through a rocky period. We feel ashamed that we can't handle the trouble and we aren't eager to share the problem with other people, especially relatives and friends. So, we feel isolated and alone in our troubles and come to the conclusion that *we're the only people on earth who are suffering.* Of course, this isn't true, but because so many people in the world go around wearing a happy-face mask in an attempt to hide their real feelings, we jump to the erroneous conclusion that they're happy and we aren't.

Another big secret of the 21st century is the fact that hard times can be an opportunity for growth and change in a positive direction. By working together, couples can find ways to improve their life and end up loving each other even more. In a crisis couples can do three things: 1) crash and burn; 2) muddle through the problem, neither losing nor gaining; 3) rise above the crisis by joining together on the same team and solving the problem.

Hard Times Are Stressful

Hard times in life generate stress for couples. *Stress* has been defined in many ways. One definition focuses on the body's response to various events in our world. When we perceive something especially threatening to us, our nervous system responds by releasing a flood of stress hormones including adrenaline and cortisol. These hormones rouse the body for emergency action. Our heart pounds faster, our muscles tighten, blood pressure rises, we breathe faster, our senses become sharper and more focused.

Stressors are those external events or changes in our life that cause an emotional or physical reaction. Different people are likely to respond to the same stressor in different ways. One person may be able to take the event or change in stride, while another may come unglued. The reaction depends on the individual's resources: personal strengths and capacities, couple and family strengths, one's ability to frame the event in a positive way, and other external resources.

Is stress good or bad? The short answer to this question is *both:* Stress can sometimes be both good and bad. Too little change or challenge in life can be a problem for a couple and a family: If we don't have enough to do in life, enough to challenge us, enough pushing on us to keep us growing, we become bored and lack motivation to do anything. On the other hand, too much stress or change in our life as a couple and family and we are likely to develop emotional and physical problems and experience feelings of discomfort and distress.

There is a middle ground when it comes to stress that seems best. The middle level of stress in life leads to feelings of engagement and excitement. We feel alive and energized, and this energy helps us function well.

Good stress may kill you as quickly as bad stress. The principle working here is that our body responds to good stress in the same way it responds to bad stress. Think back to what our body does when we perceive something threatening to us. For example, we are riding a bicycle and are out of control and know we are going to crash: Our heart pounds faster, our muscles tighten, blood pressure rises, we breathe faster, our senses become sharper and more focused.

Now, think about romantic love or commitment to a fascinating career. These are *good* stressors. But our body reacts the same way it reacted in an impending bicycle wreck: heart pounding, muscles tightening, blood pressure up, breathing faster, senses sharpened and focused. Love, career and a bicycle accident are quite similar in many ways, aren't they? Odd, but true.

The point here, if we haven't been very clear so far, is that good and exciting and meaningful things in life over the long term can be harmful for us. Too much of a good thing can be as dangerous as too many negatives.

Chronic, relentless stress that we are feeling because of an unhappy work situation can harm us in many ways, both physically and emotionally. Likewise, if we genuinely love our job but work too hard, are too busy, and can't seem to ever get off the merry-go-round, our body and mind are also stressed. It may seem strange, but many people will tell you that they have the best job in the world, and in the same breath say that they are taking medication for clinical depression. Too much of a good thing is just too much.

One husband describes the situation very well:

> I love my job! It always takes lots of my time because it's important for me to be successful in my career. But I'm working long hours and am gone in the evenings, which really makes my wife upset, I think. We seem to be fighting more all the time; she just can't understand how important it is for me to be successful. She is always after me to spend more time together. How can I satisfy my wife's expectations while meeting my career goals without jeopardizing either my work or my marriage? The stress is really hard on me, both at work and at home. I'm struggling with constant headaches, which increases my stress level no matter where I am.

The key to understanding all this is to think back to the ebb and flow of stress: too little stress, change or challenge in life doesn't work well for human beings, and too much doesn't work well, either. It is essential to find balance somewhere in the middle. *Some* stress, *some* change, *some* challenge in life is good for us, while too much stress, too much change, too much challenge in life leads to potential emotional and physical breakdown.

It is clear that a balanced approach makes the most sense. Being in this state of balance is called *eustress*. This is the positive form of stress, the form that is beneficial for the individual. Too much stress, you will remember, leads to a state of *distress*. Too much change, too much challenge, too much of a good thing in life over a long period of time leads to emotional and physical breakdown.

Sit down with your partner and talk about how to find a balance in life. What would be a good balance in life for you? What would be a good balance in life for your partner? How can you work together to find this balance and love each other even more?

What Doesn't Work When We Are Under Stress?

You may have already noted that we have not mentioned chemical solutions to human difficulties. Pouring yourself several stiff drinks when you lose your job may bring a short-lived bit of euphoria, but in the morning you still don't have a job and you may have a hangover. Solving problems and dealing effectively with stress demands that our communication skills and reasoning powers be working well. The solutions most often come when we are working together to help each other. Chemical depressants draw us away from each other and numb our capacities to find solutions to life's problems.

Self-medicating can be dangerous to a relationship:

> My husband and I don't make much money so we have a lot of stress trying to make ends meet at the end of each month. I know I nag him too often to quit drinking and we would have more money. But I'm afraid that what I am doing is causing him to drink more. Now he goes to the bar right after work and sometimes doesn't get home until late at night. I think he goes to the bar to hide his stress over finances and I drive him to stay away because I can't help but blame him for the mess we are in.

Sometimes we lean on other diversions to help us manage the stress: snacking or overeating, smoking, or using prescription drugs or illegal drugs. None of these are genuine solutions; they don't solve the problem. In fact, they often complicate life by adding other problems that cause more stress.

Common Stressful Events
Couples and Families Face

When we are having difficulties in life, we often feel as if no other person on earth has ever gone through this difficulty. As we said earlier, one explanation for this phenomenon is that we all know how to put on the mask of happiness in our daily lives and give each other the false impression that, "Life is perfect for everyone but me, hiding here behind my mask."

Researchers in the field of family studies have made it very clear, however, that there are many common stressful events for couples and families. David H. Olson, Hamilton McCubbin, and their colleagues at the University of Minnesota studied 1,000 intact families to learn more about how husbands and wives view stress in each stage of the family life cycle. Participants in the study included young couples, couples in the middle years, and couples in the later years of life. The researchers divided the families in the study into seven groups, based on where each family was in the family life cycle: young couples without children; childbearing couples; couples with school-age children; couples with adolescents in the family; couples with children about to launch from home; empty-nest couples; and couples in the retirement years.

The researchers found that:

- *Stress and strain are common* in all seven stages of the family life cycle.
- *Financial strains ranked first* in five of the seven stages of the family life cycle. Strains among family members were present in all seven stages of the family life cycle; and strains caused by work outside the home were stressful for all ages and stages.
- *A major pileup of stressors and strains* occurs during the launching period when young people are soon to be leaving home. During this time, couples report their lowest levels of family satisfaction.
- *Stress drops dramatically and family satisfaction increases* among couples in middle years and for those whose children have left home.
- *Husbands and wives are generally in agreement* in their view of the number of demands upon them. However, the researchers found that wives reported slightly more demands than husbands during four stages—childbearing, school-age children, launching, and empty nest.
- *Losing, quitting or retiring from a job.* Many families experienced considerable stress when a family member left a job, whether they were leaving by choice or by the employer's decision. Stress from leaving a job occurs in all stages of the family life cycle. It

was especially common during the young couple stage and the launching stage.

- *Illness and death in the family.* Serious illness of a family member or close relative affected about 33% of families in all stages, but was especially common in the launching and empty nest stages. Roughly 20% of the families throughout the life cycle were affected by death. This occurred most often during the launching, empty nest and retirement stages.

It should be clear by now that difficulties in life are very common. Everyone experiences hard times. Everyone endures stress and strain. Everyone suffers sometimes. Sometimes these stresses and strains are so severe that we feel we are near the breaking point.

Think back: What was the most stressful time in life that you can remember? What made this time so stressful?

Why Do Some Families Fail in a Crisis And Some Families Succeed?

The short answer to this extraordinarily important question is that some families are simply better prepared to deal with stress in their lives. They have major strengths they can rely upon to deal effectively with the inevitable challenges life brings.

Why some couples and families fail and some succeed has fascinated researchers and counselors for many years. For example, pick a crisis in life: a death in the family, loss of a job, financial difficulties, deployment of a family member in wartime, retirement, pregnancy, a health problem, a new member or members in the family. Pick any crisis in life. There are countless crises you can choose from. Some couples or families, when facing one of these crises, will be torn apart in their struggle to deal with the problem. They will fall into endless bickering, blaming each other rather than focusing on the problem, and arguing over whose fault it is. Or they will become so overwhelmed by the terrible event that has occurred that they will draw apart from each other into their own silent, individual worlds. They will each face the difficulty alone and in doing so they will be more likely to break up.

Other couples and families will spend very little time or no time at all in blaming each other or withdrawing from each other. The vast majority of their time will be invested in figuring out how to work together to rise above their difficulties. These successful families will not be asking, "Who is at fault here?"

Rather, they will be asking the question, "How can we help each other grow and become stronger as we face this challenge together?"

We all deal with stress differently, but the difference between success and failure in hard times depends on asking the right questions and then seeking steadfastly to find the right answers.

What Strengths Protect Couples and Families During Hard Times?

If a couple and a family have developed several important strengths in their relationship, they are more likely to succeed in the face of difficulties in life. We have seen that strong couples and strong families in America and around the world share six interrelated, major qualities. How can these strengths be used to help them through hard times?

- *Appreciation and Affection*. Under stress and during a crisis, people who have an abundant reserve of appreciation and affection for each other are likely to seek shelter in each other's arms, band together, care for each other when the going gets rough. As one young husband told his young wife upon learning that she had contracted a potentially disfiguring and crippling disease: "I certainly don't want this to happen to us, but you can always be certain that I will be here to push your wheelchair." Without this vast reservoir of goodwill toward each other, many of the crises couples face in life would be simply unbearable.
- *Positive Communication*. If a couple is in the habit of talking in a kind, gentle, and supportive way to each other, when hard times hit they will not be as likely to fall into a downward spiral. By practicing positive communication when life *is* going well, a couple is immunizing their relationship for protection when life *does not* go well. Plan time to be alone as a couple so you can take this time to reconnect. Keep the communication positive and your stress load will be lighter.
- *Commitment*. Couples who have a well-developed feeling of commitment toward each other are, by nature, more likely to

weather hard times. Because of this commitment, they do not have to worry about the future as much; they can be confident the other person will be there when he is needed. Commitment does not come automatically, but develops steadily and surely over time. Life brings many tests for couples and passing a difficult test together during a time of crisis helps to strengthen their commitment to each other.

- ***Enjoyable Time Together****.* We all seek shelter in a storm, and a couple who has always enjoyed being with each other will naturally look to each other for a warm, loving and comforting place to be until the storm blows over. Just hanging out together, as we commonly say today, is essential when life gets hard. Enjoying a good meal together, a good talking-and-listening session, a good cry together, a good laugh . . . having a history of doing these things in good times helps ensure that we will do them in bad times.

- ***Spiritual Well-Being and Shared Values.*** Countless people seek spiritual solace in hard times. The solace is found, for many, in the community of a church, a mosque, a synagogue. For many others a sense of hope, optimism and joy in the face of difficulty is found in nature, in prayer, in meditation, in connection with something greater than oneself. There are myriad ways this sense of connection and consolation is found. And a sense of peace is found at home in the comfort of each other's arms.

- ***The Ability to Manage Stress and Crisis Effectively.*** Strong couple and family relationships, by their very nature, are resilient and resourceful. It is important to remember that everyone deals with stress a little differently. And that is okay! Don't try to make the other person deal with stress the way you do; just understand that we don't all handle situations the same way. Couples who are gifted in managing stress in life have a wide variety of tools available to them. Research on strong families reveals many useful, positive approaches that are used to deal with stress and crises in one's life.

What Works for You ?

Try this exercise: Sit down with your partner, each with a piece of paper and a pencil. Each of you write down what you do to manage the stressors in your life. Make a list of what works well for you, personally. And, write down why each of these things on your list works well for you as an individual.

1. _____

   _____

2. _____

   _____

3. _____

   _____

4. _____

   _____

Now, after you've written down the good things that work for you when you're under stress and why these various approaches work, share your list with your partner and see how your approaches to stress are similar and how they are different. This is a great exercise for helping you as a couple to better understand each other. Be sure to make this a fun activity, not a chore or a debate.

Just Out of Curiosity, What Doesn't Work for you?

Now, in a similar fashion, what are some things that *don't* work very well for you and your partner when there is stress in your lives? We invite you to describe these things, also. What do you do that doesn't work, and why?

1. _____

_____

2. _____

_____

3. _____

_____

4. _____

_____

Again, share what you have written down with your partner. Remember: You're not doing this to find out what is wrong with each other. This is not a game of *Find and Fix*: It is a mistake to treat a loved one like a broken toy. Instead, you are simply learning important things about your partner's world and how it is similar and different from yours. This activity—looking at both what you do that works under stress and what you do that doesn't work under stress—would make a great activity for a date night. A conversation-starter.

The ABC-X Family Crisis Model

The late Reuben Hill, a pioneer in the field of family studies at the University of Minnesota, explained why some families do better than others in hard times with what he called the ABC-X Model. The model explains that:

A = the stressor event
B = the family's crisis-meeting resources
C = the definition the family gives to the event
X = the crisis

Hill defined a stressor as "a situation for which the family has had little or no prior preparation," and a crisis as "any sharp or decisive change for which old patterns are inadequate." Or, you could use the dictionary definition of a crisis as simply "a turning point in life."

As an example, think about a family in which the mother is driving to work one morning and is severely injured when a speeding driver runs a red light. The *stressor event*, A, is quite serious: a car crash causing multiple injuries to this young mother. But simply knowing that a car crash occurred and serious injury resulted does not give you a clue about how the story will unfold.

If the family possesses important *crisis-meeting resources*, B, the likelihood they will survive and manage to rise above this tragedy increases dramatically. *If* the family's crisis-meeting resources include valuable relationship strengths among the members, *if* the family has adequate financial resources, health insurance and access to high-quality medical facilities, *if* the family is connected to supportive people at work, in the community, and among their own extended family . . . There are literally countless ifs, but the more valuable crisis-meeting resources the family can draw upon, the better.

C, *the definition the family gives to this event*, also plays an important part in how the crisis unfolds. When families find some good to hold onto in a tragic situation and they can find a way to look to the future and grow together, the likelihood of a more positive resolution to X, *the crisis*, is likely.

Once again we ask the question, "Why do some families fail in a crisis and some families succeed?" The ABC-X Model helps us understand that it is not just the stressor event but the interaction of the event with the family's strengths, the resources they can tap, and how they think about the situation that all combine to determine how severe the crisis becomes in their lives. This helps us better understand how some couples and families rise above the trauma they face, while others sink.

Life as a Roller Coaster

Reuben Hill also observed that how a family deals with stress and crisis can look something like a roller coaster ride. Life has its ups and downs as we all know, and a family dealing with stress and crisis in their lives gets caught up in the ride. Let's go back to the young mother who was severely injured in the car crash. Here is one example from many possibilities of how the crisis could turn out: Right before the crash, as she is driving to work, she is thinking about how wonderful her life is; seconds later she is broad-sided by a speeding driver and her life and the life of her family is turned upside-down. She almost dies on two occasions in the hospital; the rest of the immediate family—dad, sister, brother, grandparents—are thrown into despair, thinking she will die, and there is disorder as they try to adjust to all the changes in life caused by the incapacity of their mother and wife. She endures two surgeries and slowly starts to recover; however, a third reconstructive surgery is ultimately required. Three months later, she is out of the hospital and receiving rehabilitation services. Most important, she has returned to the shelter of her loving family. Through all the difficulties, they strive to care for her the very best way they can.

Now, fast-forward to four years later. She is almost fully recovered from the accident. Four years after the crash, however, the family has found *a new normal* in life, rather than the normal they used to experience. Mom, partially disabled, recently found a new job. Everyone loves and values each other more than before the catastrophe. No longer do they take other family members for granted. Now they have learned they are all holding onto a very slender thread and they want to cherish the moment because moments don't last forever.

How Does *Your* Roller Coaster Ride Look?

On the following page, we have sketched out a very simplified version of how the young mother and her family might draw the roller coaster ride they had been on as they recovered from the car crash and her terrible injuries. Before the crash life was looking up. At the point of the crash it was as if they all fell off a cliff together. Their happy world was plunged into emotional despair. Then through the long process of recovery through the months and years they gathered together, they gained strength from each other, and four years later they had actually risen above the disaster in many ways and were even happier than they were before the car crash. (See Figure 13-1.)

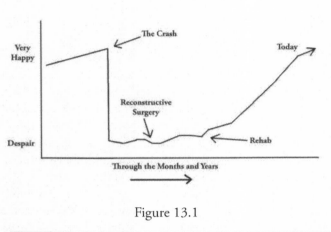

Figure 13.1

You and your family also have been passengers on the roller coaster of life. Below is a blank graph. Think about the challenging time you and your family have faced together. Chart on the graph the ups and downs you experienced and note important events in this journey. (See Figure 13-2.)

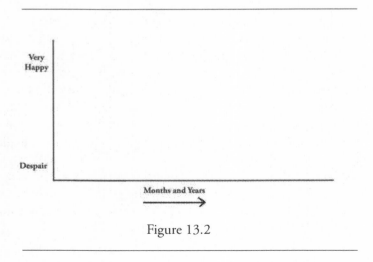

Figure 13.2

As you look back over this long ride, what were the key elements in your success in recovering from the crisis? If you wish, write them down below:

_____

_____

_____

_____

Severe Couple and Family Problems

Because families are remarkably resilient and know how to work together through hard times, they can deal successfully with the vast majority of stressors they face in life. There are, however, some problems that demand intervention and help from outside the family. You will remember the fellow who could clearly distinguish between those challenges he could handle and those problems that demanded extra expertise and help: " . . . I'll never be able to perform brain surgery on myself if I need it. . . ."

Especially difficult couple and family problems that are often outside the capacity of those inside the family to resolve include:

- alcohol and other drug problems
- physical abuse
- emotional abuse
- sexual abuse
- mental health issues
- disabilities
- major illnesses
- a death in the family

Couples and families simply cannot solve these problems by themselves and need to seek insight and support from professionals in the community. Skilled support from trained volunteers working in countless support groups can also be especially helpful.

***Remember*:** There are professionals skilled to work with any couple and family problem imaginable. And, there are support groups offering their services for little cost or none at all for every difficulty people can possibly face in life.

If you don't have a clue where to go for ideas, talk with people in your life that you trust: relatives, friends, colleagues at work, and so forth. A quick visit to the Internet will find many different resources in your community or the surrounding area that can be of service.

Preventing Major Problems in Life

Back to where we began: Everyone suffers in life. Everyone experiences stress, everyone will endure severe crises in life. Difficulties in life are inevitable. As one very wise grandmother said, not long before she died: "Life *is* problems. That's just the way it goes."

This wise woman had suffered through poverty, cold, hunger and pain, the loss of two babies, and through several bouts of domestic violence. She watched two sons and a son-in-law go off to war. All three came home, but one was emotionally scarred for the rest of his life. She suffered through the ravages of advanced diabetes, including several progressive surgical amputations that left her without either of her legs. First, a foot was amputated; then the other. Next, up to the knee. Then up to the other knee. Finally, both legs were amputated completely. She ended her life bedridden and the diabetes had ruined her eyes.

But she was certainly not blind to the realities of life—both the good and the bad. Her spirit certainly was not broken. And she retained her inherent goodness as a human being.

At the very end of her life, she was still a serene, pleasant, warm and basically happy person. Life to her inevitably had problems with which to deal. She could not prevent all the major problems that she faced in life. She knew that sometimes one has the power to prevent these big problems from happening, but more often, one does not have the power.

More importantly, she had learned that even if you cannot stop something from happening, you *can* control how you respond to the crisis. And that is the key: Make sure that you do not make things worse for yourself and others, and seek to make the situation better for yourself and those you love.

The key for her was to invest in her family, build lifelong relationships, and speak openly and honestly with the people she loved and trusted.

Stressors are those external events or changes in our life that cause an emotional or physical reaction. As we have seen, people are likely to respond to the same stressor in many different ways. One person may be able to take the event or change in stride, while another may come unglued. The reaction depends on the individual's resources: personal strengths and capacities, couple and family strengths, and one's ability to frame the event in a positive way.

In the words of one young woman, "The way you think is how you live. If your thoughts are negative, that is how you will approach a crisis in your life. If you think positively, you will approach the situation in a positive way."

How do you respond to life? Do you see only the bad, or do you look for the good?

If we strive every day to nurture and develop our couple and family strengths, we will lead happier, healthier, more satisfying and more meaningful lives. The strengths we enjoy as a couple and as a family will be a wonderful immunization against the inevitable stressor events and crises that occur in everyone's lives.

Very Short Stories from Real People

That appreciation and affection stuff really works! My husband and I were getting to the place that if he wasn't going to do things for me and be nice, then I wasn't going to be nice to him. Then I read about how appreciation and affection can make a relationship work. So, I tried to be appreciative and show some affection to my husband even if he seemed like he ignored me. Well, it took a day or so, but then he started to respond the same, a little at a time. I think we both were getting stressed because neither of us was showing appreciation to the other, so we were building distance into the relationship. How foolish!

I was sexually abused as a child by my father for a number of years. My mother knew about it but was afraid he would kill her if she tried to rescue me. I finally escaped from that life when I was 17. I ran away from home with a guy who was 27. That turned out poorly, as you can expect, but it did get me away from my father. I stumbled through life, bitter and depressed for several years, but there were also good people along the way. After lots of mistakes, I finally learned how to connect with good people and stay away from those who would harm me. Today I'm married and have two beautiful little girls. I have a great job working with children with disabilities and a husband who loves me. Sometimes I still wake up in the middle of the night and sob, but life is getting steadily better and I find help from many good people who care about me.

In a four-year period of our life it seemed like the bottom fell out of everything. My wife's elderly mother went steadily downhill, in and out of the hospital. As her mother faded, my wife lost weight and got so worn down I thought she might die before her mother died. While this was going on, our daughter became very ill after she lost a baby. Her struggle with depression lasted a couple of years. To me, it's always the worst when something bad happens to your kids. During this time, I ended up in the hospital for several days and had surgery. While I was home trying to recover, my mother was hospitalized and died a few weeks after that. One more surgery for me followed 18 months later. During this four-year period all of us experienced despair and emotional exhaustion. It was a dreadful time. And yet, I never once thought that our family would break under the pressure. And I never once thought our marriage would end. We had been through many other difficulties in life in the early days of our marriage and these had prepared us for the worst. I believe in strong, happy families, because we have one.

———❖———

I grew up and learned from my family that the glass was always half-empty. My husband grew up in a family that thought the glass was always half-full. One of the reasons I fell in love with him was because of that half-full glass he always had with him. That's one really important thing he has taught me over the years. It took awhile for me to learn how to look at the world in a more positive way, but I did it!

Discussion Questions

1. Is your life well-balanced? Do you have enough happening to keep you feeling alive and energized? Or, do you have too much to do? Do you feel overwhelmed? Talk with your partner about how each of you feel. Find a way to work together and help bring both of your lives into balance.
2. What was the most stressful time in life that you can remember? What made this time so stressful? What did you and your loved ones do to help make life better during this difficult time?
3. How are being in love, having a career, and experiencing a bicycle accident similar?

Tips for Strengthening Your Relationship

1. We have an expectation that we can *do it all,* but we can't. It's just not realistic. Work at making your expectations reasonable to lower your stress level.
2. Communicate with your spouse when that stressful feeling creeps up. Sometimes just talking about it will decrease your anxiety.
3. Recognize good stress and bad stress in your life and work on finding a balance for the good stress, so it doesn't turn bad.
4. Agree to *fight fair.* Each partner takes time to listen to the feelings of the other before speaking. *Respond,* which requires thinking, instead of just *reacting* with impulsive feelings.

5. After a stressful event is successfully navigated, celebrate! Take time to have a stress-free date night, even if that is just renting a movie. Turn the lights down, snuggle and enjoy.

6. We can't have it all, and we can't do it all. Instead, we need to develop more realistic expectations for ourselves and our loved ones, so that we can lower our stress level.

7. When couples learn how to laugh together and cry together in good times and bad, they develop a bond that keeps them close through thick and thin.

8. It's okay to feel angry about something. It's not okay to take your anger out on other people. Let people know how you feel but don't blame everyone else.

9. Surround yourself with loved ones and friends you can rely on during stressful times. And be a person others can rely upon to help when they need help.

CHAPTER 14

Stepfamilies: Can Different Family Cultures Be Blended Together?

Stepfamilies are the moral pioneers of contemporary family life, showing us all how to love and persevere in the face of loyalties that multiply and divide, but never fully converge.

William Doherty

Divorced or widowed parents with children from previous marriages or relationships who cohabitate, or legally remarry are called stepfamilies. There are many other terms that are used to describe these families, including: *combined families, re-coupled families, complicated families, binuclear families, merged families, integrated families, secondary families, reconstituted families* and *blended families*. With so many different terms used for stepfamilies, it is clear that they spark a great deal of interest and discussion in our society.

Ninety percent of stepfamilies are formed after one or both partners have experienced a divorce. The remaining percentage of stepfamilies are formed when one spouse dies and the remaining parent remarries, or by an out-of-wedlock birth and a subsequent marriage by one of the parents.

Besides the term *stepfamily*, the most commonly used term for this remarried family is probably the term *blended family*. Many observers object to this term, however, arguing that the process is more like putting puzzle pieces together than a *blending* of individuals. Human beings never really blend together, always retaining their individuality and uniqueness, and this is good.

Whichever term is used to describe this family type, it is important to remember that this nontraditional new family structure has been formed with the hope of starting a new life together following the loss and hurt of a previous family structure.

This process of coming together is not simple. It's not just two adults who love each other simply and smoothly becoming a new family. Having children involved complicates matters. Every couple in a stepfamily starts with high hopes of a new beginning for love, loyalty and stability. However, the hopes and expectations of the child may not be the same as those of the newly-marrying couple.

As far back as Greek and Roman times more than 2,000 years ago, there were stories of stepfamilies, and many of these stories were not all that positive. Likewise, fairy tales from Northern Europe dating back several centuries also put stepfamilies in a very negative light: fighting and blaming each other, dominated by wicked stepparents, and crowded with worthless stepchildren. These stories throughout history tell us that stepfamilies have faced challenges for a long time.

Stepfamily Statistics

How common are stepfamilies today? Divorce rates in the U.S. have remained stable for more than 20 years, with about one divorce for every two marriages. Nearly 50% of marriages are a remarriage for at least one partner, according to the National Healthy Marriage Resource Center. U.S. Census Bureau statistics reported by the Stepfamily Foundation indicate that 1,300 new stepfamilies are formed every day in this country. An estimated one in three weddings creates a new stepfamily. And data reported by the National Stepfamily Resource Center indicate that 30% of all children in the U.S. are likely to spend some time in a stepfamily before they are 18 years old. Keeping these numbers in mind, we will concentrate on the ways to strengthen the stepfamily relationships.

Many people remarry within two or three years of their divorce. Thus, individuals often do not take the time or make the effort to figure out why their first marriage failed before they are involved in a new relationship that may be on the road to a second marriage. This helps to explain why the divorce rate for second and third marriages is significantly higher than the divorce rate for first marriages. Less than 25% of remarrying couples seek premarital preparation, so they hit the ground running and often don't have the time to devote to developing the new couple relationship, which is the foundation for a stepfamily's strengths, according to Ron Deal and David H. Olson.

Getting Off to a Good Start

To succeed as a stepfamily, the couple must find ways to keep their relationship as the number one priority in the family, the foundation for everything else. Without this strong relationship in place, stress from raising children, former spouses, job demands, health issues and finances can all combine, causing the partnership and the stepfamily to fail.

According to the U.S. Census Bureau, 60% of second marriages end in divorce. The first two years of this new marriage have proven to be critical for the couple in many cases. It is important to get the marriage off to a good start, and to encourage the growth of stepfamily strengths, children should be included in opportunities for family decision making as often as possible.

When children have previously lived with both biological parents, they bring the memories of the absent parent into the new stepparent-stepchild relationship. This is especially true when a parent has died. Stepparents may have to overcome the obstacle of this *invisible* parent in every scenario related to trust, loyalty and discipline. This invisible parent is especially an obstacle when children fear a new relationship with the stepparent means a loss of loyalty to the absent parent. The wise stepparent will accept these elusive comparisons to the past by encouraging the child to talk about these feelings and assuring the child there is no desire to take the place of the biological parent. The stepparent also will need to recognize this behavior as a defense mechanism by the child to keep the stepparent relationship from growing closer. Children sometimes worry that by coming closer to the stepparent they will be distancing themselves from the absent biological parent, or the memory of that parent. The passage of time and continued effort to build a trusting relationship will help this issue fade away.

It also takes time for the members of new stepfamilies to learn about each other's histories, negotiate new traditions and create their own family memories. Two existing family cultures are trying to fit together into one. Each member of the new family comes with a set of expectations of what *family* means and the roles ascribed to each person from their previous family culture. The birth order of the children in a stepfamily may change by the simple exchange of their parents' wedding vows! For example, if I was the oldest child in my original family and had responsibilities and privileges of an oldest child, do I lose my rank if a new stepsibling is older? Do I suddenly and automatically become the babysitter if I now have younger stepsiblings? Who is responsible for me and to whom am I responsible? These are big changes in the life of a child, and change for people of any age is confusing and stressful.

Discipline. Building a shared parenting role for discipline is one of the most important couple activities to develop early in the new family unit. It is hard to raise children in any family, but taking the role of a spouse without the real authority of a parent can be a tricky job for a stepparent: "You aren't my mother!" a child is likely to say.

Although it is usually believed that in the first two years any actual discipline needs to be delivered by the biological parent, the stepparent should be responsible on a day-to-day basis for re-enforcing and keeping the consequences of the rules established by the family group. Drs. Les and Leslie Parrott call this "living on borrowed power." This type of power is much like the power that paid caregivers have when coming into your house to care for the children. The stepparent has the authority to make rules, re-enforce rules, and discipline within the guidelines and direction agreed upon with the biological parent. It is important for the stepparent to use this borrowed power in the new family relationship to establish a consistent shared couple discipline of all children who live within the walls of the family home at any time. This eliminates an opportunity for the children to manipulate the situation until the other parent gets home.

Healing, time, planning and effort. A successful stepfamily does not happen by accident and it does not happen overnight. It takes planning, intelligence and goodwill on the part of those who are involved. According to family researchers Betty Carter and Monica McGoldrick, people go through three major stages in the process of creating a new family through remarriage: (1) entering a new relationship; (2) planning the new marriage and family, and (3) developing a stepfamily.

Before beginning the first stage, *entering a new relationship*, divorced individuals should feel that they have recovered from the loss of their first marriage; widowed individuals should allow time for healing. If they have not done this, they risk "marrying on the rebound." But to be successful in the new relationship, one must be divorced or recovered emotionally as well as legally from the first partner. This process of recovery and resolution of the first marriage can take a long time.

During the second stage in the formation of a stepfamily, *planning the new marriage and family*, both spouses-to-be and their children must learn to accept their own fears about the new marriage and the formation of a stepfamily. During this period of time it is also important to accept the fact that much time and patience are needed to adjust to the complexity and unknown habits of a new family. It is not going to be an easy process. Besides adjusting to new roles as a new spouse, new stepparent, new stepchild, and a new member of a new extended family, the family members also need to make adjustments in terms of space, time, membership and authority. They also need to deal with emotional issues, including feelings of guilt, loyalty conflicts, the desire for closeness to both the new children and the biological children, and unresolvable past hurts. One stepfather lamented that he spent so much time, money and energy on his new spouse and her children that he was neglecting his own children from the previous marriage.

During the third stage, *developing a stepfamily*, the newly married partners need to strengthen their couple relationship so that they can function effectively as co-parents. All family members need to realize that the new marriage is a genuine family that the couple is trying to build together. During this phase, room has to be made in the new family for stepchildren, half-siblings, new sets of grandparents and extended kin. It is also important to make room for relationships among all the children and their biological (noncustodial) parents, grandparents and other extended family members. Sharing memories and histories from each side of the new stepfamily can help in building this new family.

As we have noted before, when you marry you do not marry an individual. You marry a whole family that comes with this individual. Similarly, when you remarry and form a stepfamily, you are connecting two already-formed and complex families. Again, this is a challenging task because the number of relationships between family members multiplies as the number of family members increases.

Unrealistic expectations. Human beings often expect too much too soon. Unrealistic expectations of family members can create conflict in any family, but in the stepfamily these can be especially detrimental to the formation of a strong family unit. *Instant love* is often desired and expected by some members of the new family unit, but it is unrealistic to think this will happen. All relationships take time to develop and the relationships in the stepfamily have to deal with two separate family units overlapping through the children. These transitions often increase loyalty issues in regard to the biological parent. Children now struggle with deciding which parent has the most right to tell them what to do, who they will allow to love them and who they will choose to love in return. Adults have a very difficult time figuring out love. Imagine how difficult it must be for children.

Making Parenting Time Work

In the stepfamily, the comings and goings of children to different homes for parenting time can be a full-time scheduling nightmare. In a new family unit where both parents have children from a previous marriage, it is highly unlikely that they will have the same visitation schedules for children unless there is excellent communication and a low level of conflict with the child's other parent. Are both parents' children going to be in the home on the same weekend? Will one parent send her or his children to spend time with the other biological parent so the children alternate weekends? Will all of the children belonging to both parents spend the weekend together?

Day-to-day, a stepchild may be well-adjusted as the only child, the youngest child or the oldest child until the children of the new parent come for parenting time and roles shift. Once again, it is important to note that a balancing act can be accomplished but it is very unlikely that everyone will be pleased. Somebody is usually going to feel as if Goldilocks is sitting in her/his chair, eating her/his porridge!

When the biological children come to share parenting time with their father or mother, the stepparent's attention naturally shifts to her or his biological children and this may be perceived as bias by the stepchildren. The children living day-to-day in the stepfamily are likely to experience confusion and also have a feeling that they are less important in the stepparent's life than the biological children. This often becomes a no-win situation for the stepparent as he or she tries to assure all the children that they are loved and cared for equally. It is true that a stepparent coping with a headstrong nonbiological child or with a teenager who refuses to cooperate may seem like a nightmare. Stepparents who take the time for consistent nurturing and open communication will increase the chances of a strong stepparent-stepchild relationship. Research conducted by the Stepfamily Association of America (which has evolved today into the National Stepfamily Resource Center) indicates that this may take several years to achieve depending on the ages of children at the time of the stepfamily commitment.

It is natural for a teenager to feel a closer bond with her or his own biological parents than with a stepparent. Teens act on the independence that they have learned throughout their life, and they will definitely rely on this in the stepfamily situation. Teens use their fierce loyalty to the biological noncustodial parent to shield themselves from having to let down their guard and build a new relationship with a stepparent. They fear that they will be disloyal by relating to the stepparent as a *parent* when they already have two parents, thank you, and don't need or want anymore adults ruling their lives!

Younger children learn boundaries by hearing what parents say and by watching parental actions. Younger children are often torn about parenting time with the noncustodial parent because they might breach the boundaries set in place by the stepfamily. The rule that is often spoken to younger children is, "What happens in this house stays in this house." (This is not to be confused with abusive parents who want children to keep secrets.) The children probably heard this phrase repeated many times going back and forth between the biological parents. Divorced parents often put the children in the middle by asking them to act as a spy at the other parent's house, but they don't want children to share what goes on in their house.

As the children go back and forth for their parenting time with the stepfamily and with the other biological parent, miscommunication and controversy are likely to arise. It is important for parents to have age-appropriate discussions with the children focusing on the importance of boundaries and maintaining privacy. Children can create a great deal of conflict through manipulation if they don't honor the boundaries in both homes.

Building Quality Time

It would be ideal if all of the children would visit their other parent's home on the same weekend, leaving the newly married couple time alone to enhance the couple relationship. It is important to find time to do this, whenever possible.

In one family we know this was seen as the date weekend for the parents. They had candlelight dinners at home, slept late and generally doted on each other while doing the laundry, cleaning the house and running errands. As they noted, "It sounds rather boring, but gosh was it exciting to do all those things without kids underfoot!"

If only one set of children at a time visits the noncustodial parent, it gives the new stepparent time to form a bond with her or his stepchildren. This can be a great time for this family to establish a special ritual. Of course, to be fair the ritual will be repeated the next weekend with the other children in the marriage. William J. Doherty, a professor of family social science at the University of Minnesota-St. Paul, states in his book *The Intentional Family* that repeated rituals shared between stepchild and stepparent can slowly build a one-on-one relationship. This ritual might be a breakfast for two, a shopping trip for just the two family members or perhaps a camping trip together.

One family designated a job jar and each weekend everyone pulled out a job from the jar, completed the job and then the family went out to breakfast. When they returned home they played board games, watched movies, played a computer game or had fun outside. During the sports season the kids might have a game on the weekend and the family would build their *family date* around that event. Spending quality time together created a special bond with the children.

The Strength of Communication

The stepparent learns quickly to invite children to talk about all of their parents in an atmosphere of acceptance or the child just will not engage in the conversation. Parents are often struck by fear and jealousy. They fear the children will want to leave the stepfamily to live with the other biological parent. Or, in the case of widowed parents, the idealized "invisible" parent was the perfect parent. These are common issues and need to be discussed openly in families. Don't be afraid of this type of conversation. Encourage the children to talk about their feelings. "I would really like to hear why you would like to move in with your dad." "I would like to know how you feel your parent would have handled this situation." Make sure these are quiet, calm, respectful conversations about what is making them feel this way. It is important to set the stage for family communication.

Anger at remarriage, a poor relationship with the new stepparent or stepsibling rivalry could all be a part of the desire for children to want to change residence from one parent to the other. Of course, the parenting plan is still the legal guide for custody, but it is possible if the communication between biological parents is good and conflict is low to work through this together without court intervention. Working it out between the ex-spouses can be a lot simpler and cheaper than going to court, if both agree to be reasonable and work in the best interests of the kids.

If it becomes clear that there is a genuine issue, work with it. Don't try to ignore or avoid it. If the behavior is manipulative to get back at the biological parent for remarrying, then recognize it, encourage the child to recognize it and work together for a new set of expectations so all family members feel honored and accepted. Family mediation programs in your community are often good places to get unbiased negotiation on these types of issues. Their job is not to be on any particular individual's side, but on the side of strengthening the family's relationships with each other.

Because communication is the major part of any relationship, stepfamilies can benefit by learning how to discuss matters without sounding like they are blaming or scolding each other. By removing the word *You* from the start of the discussion and using the word *I*, many conflicts can be avoided and messages can be accurately understood. The following tips for using *I Messages* may help. (See <u>Box 14-1</u>.)

Positive Communication:
How to Communicate Without Scolding
and Blaming

I Messages are used to express the feelings of the speaker in a nonthreatening way, without blame. If you start scolding or blaming a child, you're likely to get into a hopeless battle.

An easy way to think about *I Messages* is F.B.I. (Feelings+Behavior+Intention).

Here are several examples of F.B.I. *I Messages:*

I feel confused about why you are so angry with me that you want to go live with your dad/mom. Can we talk about your thoughts?

I feel so proud of you for sharing your room with the other kids when they come for the weekend. Do you have some ideas about how to make this easier for you and them?

I feel very happy that you invited me to go to your basketball game. Do you think we could get something to eat and talk about all of the great plays you made?

I feel confused that you told your dad/mom that I yell at you. Next time you feel that I am yelling at you, please tell me how you feel.

Compared to the family before the divorce, the complexity of the stepfamily is important to discuss. Now there are parents, stepparents, grandparents, step-grandparents, siblings, stepsiblings, plus all of the other aunts, uncles, cousins and friends. If you like lots of commotion and interaction with lots of people, a stepfamily will make you happy! Being open to new traditions and expectations can make your life rich with memories and experiences. If you are closed to these opportunities, you will lose the chance to grow and expand your relationship experiences.

Stepfamilies *do* have strengths. Take time to explore your strengths together.

Very Short Stories of Stepfamily Strengths

> At our wedding, we included the children of both families who wished to be a part of the ceremony. Everyone had a new outfit to wear and they were pretty excited because we had given them the opportunity to be a part of a commitment ceremony. After the wedding vows were completed, the family commitment ceremony took place with vows by the children to uphold the new family through prayer, communication and commitment to new traditions. Each person received a family medal as a symbol of our commitment. The children are now adults and their medals hang prominently in their bedrooms. This didn't mean that there were never hard times. There were many hard times, but we all made the commitment to work it out as a family. Some issues took longer and more outside intervention from professionals to help solve, but we did it and we still do it together.

> Couch Time was the first rule that my family developed. Every night after dinner, everyone, including the dog, gathered on the couch. It was during this time that the family just talked over the day or read books together or sometimes played a board game at the table. Family meetings are often talked about as ways to keep families in tune with what is working and what isn't. In my family, the kids said, "Why do we have to have a meeting? We're a family not a business!" Couch Time was relaxed enough to provide us the time to talk about all of the same things without seeming so formal.

Today, the kids are in their 30s and when they come home, we still have Couch Time. These times together went a long way to help us develop a sense of appreciation and affection for each other. We now enjoy hanging out together because we really like each other.

———◄●►———

The invisible parent (in our situation, the parent who had died), was very real, especially at times when one of the children did not like how life was going for him. In their young minds, the invisible parent was the perfect parent and would allow them to do whatever they wanted to do. We often talked about that parent and how we really did not know how that parent would have handled the situation, but yet assured the child that life probably would not have been much different than what they were currently experiencing. As time went on, and everyone became better adjusted to the new family, the invisible parent became less of an issue.

———◄●►———

My son is diabetic. He was 13 and a typical angry teenager. We were about three years into our stepfamily unit. When he became diabetic, my son blamed me. He actually acquired it from a virus, not genetically. This was really his anger at the divorce and the disease that was coming out in the disguise of blame for the illness.

Many times he was in intensive care and Mom, Dad and Stepdad would be there together by his side. There was no conflict between parents. Our unity on the issue of getting our son through the crisis was apparent to him.

His stepdad supported him financially, emotionally and spiritually. My son would often be surly and ignore his stepdad. This continued throughout high school, a very long time for our stepfamily. We wondered if he would ever change his attitude toward his stepdad. It took a couple of more unplanned crises to make this young man realize that his stepfather loved him, stood beside him and suffered with him through every choice he made. They are now very good adult friends.

My blended family came as a result of the deaths of our first spouses. At Christmastime the first year we were married, we got out all our Christmas decorations, and let the kids decorate. Interestingly, the next year they remembered where each item had been placed the year before and insisted that it be done the same! Our new family traditions had already begun!

When the children were younger, we took several family vacations. At the time, we weren't always sure they appreciated seeing things like Yellowstone—"You mean, you have to get out of the van to see Old Faithful?"—and similar wonders of nature. Interestingly, to celebrate our 25th anniversary, our now-adult children have planned a return trip for all of us—now with spouses and grandchildren included!—to one of our favorite places, a cabin in Arkansas.

Discussion Questions

1. What kind of planning have you done to make your stepfamily successful?
2. What are the most difficult issues you face as a stepfamily?
3. What are some topics that you won't discuss with either your children or your stepchildren?
4. What are some activities that you can do as a couple to strengthen your relationship?
5. What new family traditions could your stepfamily establish?
6. What are some of the strengths of your stepfamily?

Tips for Strengthening Stepfamily Relationships

1. Make the couple relationship the center of your family.
2. Spend time every day, if possible, but at least once a week alone together. Just you and your biological child.
3. Start a new family tradition by spending special time with each of the stepchildren daily or at least once each week to build trust and friendship.
4. Find opportunities to build new traditions and activities while respecting old ones.
5. Have family meals together at least once a day with rich discussion.
6. Set boundaries on topics that you won't discuss with the children, such as the other parent or the stepparent.
7. Create and post family rules with input from each member of the new family.
8. Be sure that every child has a *personal space*, even if it is a basket in the closet for her/his things.
9. Work successfully at blending *yours and mine* before having a baby.
10. Make a plan for visiting extended family members.
11. When the children are old enough to understand, work together as a family to make a family budget that everyone can understand.
12. Allow children to talk about the *invisible parent*.
13. Let each child grieve the loss of the parent in his or her own way and time. However, if a child's well-being is affected, don't hesitate to get professional help.

CHAPTER 15

Where do we go from here?
The Future of Our Relationship,
The Future of Our Family

Growing Together Through the Months and Years

Even the happiest of marriages have their ups and downs. Research on *great marriages*—relationships in which the couples report that they are happy with each other, love each other, are satisfied with the relationship and often consider themselves to be *best friends*—even in these very strong partnerships there can be some extraordinarily difficult periods.

For example, a study conducted at Utah State University at Logan and the University of Nebraska–Lincoln focused on couples who believed that they had created a great marriage over the years. Sarah Tulane, Linda Skogrand and John DeFrain found that more than one in four of these couples at some time in their marriage had considered divorce on at least one occasion (25 couples out of 91, or 27%, had discussed the possibility of divorce). What we can conclude from this is that even for many of the most successful couples, married life is not always likely to be a bed of roses.

Fortunately, as you will recall, a crisis in marital life together can be a catalyst for growth. Good things can come from bad situations.

But, an ounce of prevention is better than a pound of cure. So, in this chapter of the book, we will discuss preventive ways that are useful to strengthen couple relationships. And, in the event of a marital crisis, we will take a look at marital and family therapy and the importance of getting high-quality professional help when needed.

The difference between success and failure in hard times depends on asking the right questions and then seeking steadfastly to find the right answers.

The Specific Things Couples and Families Do Day-by-Day to Ensure a Meaningful And Happy Life Together

There have been innumerable studies of how couples and families successfully manage the stressors they face in everyday life together and how they endure severe crises when they arise. These very specific approaches to living ensure that couples and families do not create problems for themselves, and also work well to minimize the difficulties they face when the world thrusts problems upon them:

1—Strong families and happy couples look for something positive and focus on it. For thousands of years, people have seen hard times as being both dangerous and difficult, but also full of opportunity. In a period of crisis in their life, they look for something positive and hold onto it. Counselors call this *reframing* the situation. People seek to look at the situation in a different light, from a different angle, through a different lens. This ancient Japanese *haiku*, a form of lyric verse, is an example of reframing:

> *Since my house burned down*
> *I now own a better view*
> *of the rising moon.*

2—Strong families and happy couples pull together rather than pull apart. Strong families don't see a problem as an individual's problem but as a challenge for everyone and a reason for everyone to work together. When the young wife said to her very troubled husband, "Everything that happens to you happens to me," she meant that she shared his pain, his burden, and then the joy of helping him rise above the difficulty he was facing.

3—Strong families and happy couples are wise enough to look for help from others when they need it. They understand that some problems are much bigger, more difficult and require aid from outside. They find help from a variety of sources: from their spouse, their parents, their children, extended family members, supportive friends, neighbors, coworkers, members of a religious community and professionals in their community. "I'm smart enough to know that I can't fix the brakes on my car by myself. I can't do my income taxes. I can't cure my asthma and I'll never be able to do heart surgery on myself if I need it. So, why would I think I could solve my wife's alcohol problems? These are the reasons I go to Al-Anon."

4—Strong families and happy couples listen to each other and talk with each other. When hard times come, couples need to open up and share their thoughts and feelings. Nothing good can happen until people really start talking and listening to each other. Problems can't be fixed until they are openly discussed. And, counselors often comment that, "Anything mentionable is manageable." Meaning that if you can find the courage to talk about something, you can find the strength and ingenuity to deal with it.

5—Strong families and happy couples keep things in perspective. One young man, Allan, gained this perspective from his grandfather, whom he remembered as a very kind old gentleman. The grandfather had been an immigrant to America, escaping poverty and misery in Russia and coming to this country to find a better life for himself and his family. Years later when his grandson Allan would get depressed about how difficult his own life was, he would think back about his grandfather and all the troubles he faced: no money, scrambling to find a way to take a boat to America, not knowing the language, being beaten up in a railroad strike, being laid off of work for three years during the Great Depression, on and on and on. "If Grandpa John could get through all of these things and still be a kind and smiling man, I certainly can."

6—Strong families and happy couples adopt new roles in a flexible manner. To continue the story, during Grandpa John's time in the Depression of the 1930s, the ideal family situation was for the mother to stay home with the children and keep house, while the father worked and brought home good earnings. When Grandpa John lost his job in the Depression, however, Grandma Lottie found a job cleaning houses for rich people in the city and Grandpa John became, in effect, a househusband. He did much of the cooking and cleaning at home and learned to enjoy taking care of the couple's two daughters. The daughters, who were young adults during the Depression, did odd jobs in the city to earn money for clothes and other expenses while they were going to school. This story demonstrates role flexibility: In a difficult situation, each member of the family steps forward and does what needs to be done. The family's problems will not be solved by one individual but need to be solved by all working together.

7—Strong families and happy couples know how to compartmentalize their worries and pain. In a critical time, it is often necessary to set one's worries and sadness aside for a time and focus on basic survival. A young mother of three girls lost her husband, who died of brain cancer at age 37. Money was in short supply so she was forced back into the workplace. She was terribly lonely, having lost the best friend she ever had in life, but she knew she had to keep going for the sake of her daughters. "So, I would tough it out. I'd go to work and smile and work efficiently and effectively. And I'd come home and fix dinner and help the girls with their homework. I'd get them to bed and then I'd crawl into bed myself and snuggle up with the photograph albums full of pictures of Alex and all of us. And I would cry myself to sleep, night after night." This continued for many months until one evening, "I forgot to cry." But she remembered to cry the next night and several nights after that. And then, a night came again when "I forgot to cry." And her emotional life started to move along in a happier mode. She still misses Alex today, but is doing well in life and the girls are happy. She did not run away from her pain and loneliness. She did not try to mask it or bury it along with her husband. Rather, she recognized her genuine despair and the fact that she had a right to feel that way. But instead of letting the despair overwhelm her, she put it in a manageable box: She faced each day with strength, and ended each day honoring her husband and the pain she felt from losing him.

8—Strong families and happy couples eat well, exercise, love each other, get adequate sleep and nurture their spirit. In stressful times we often make the mistake of working harder rather than being wiser. Difficult times in life are debilitating physically and emotionally, and the no-pain-no-gain approach is not the answer. Pushing-pushing-pushing leads to physical and emotional breakdown, pure and simple.

During stressful times, it is especially necessary to do all the important things we already know we should do:

1. Eat well-balanced meals—and eat these meals together as a couple/family.
2. Exercise routinely.
3. Love each other and keep emotional bonds strong.
4. Get adequate sleep.
5. Reserve some quiet time as an individual, to nourish one's spirit.

9—*Strong families and happy couples create a life full of meaning and purpose.* Everyone faces severe crises in life. Some crises can be avoided, while others are inevitable. To be best prepared for these hard times that will hit us all, it is important to be creating a useful life of service in our family and community. This brings a richness and dignity to our lives. It strengthens us and gives us hope during the troubles we are forced to endure. Karl Menninger, a world-renowned psychiatrist, would commonly tell distressed individuals at his clinic in Topeka, Kansas, that he recommended they find good things to do in life. Rather than spend all their time feeling sorry for themselves, he would tell those who were clearly capable of doing so, "Go across the tracks. Go where people are hurting and in need and find a way to help them so that their burden is lessened." Menninger's strategy of helping others often brought comfort to the helper.

10—*Strong families and happy couples actively meet challenges head-on.* Troubles are like cars. They don't usually fix themselves. But oddly enough, people often waste a lot of time thinking that health problems, money problems, relationship problems, whatever problems they face, will somehow fix themselves. Though on rare occasions, this seems to happen almost magically, most problems need active intervention. Couples need to work together with confidence to meet the difficulties they face. Sometimes it is important to withdraw for a time from the source of the storm. Spend some time hunkered down, rest and replenish ourselves, which is different than running away from our problems. It is simply rebuilding our strength so we can come back stronger and wiser.

11—*Strong families and happy couples know how to go with the flow to some degree.* In the face of many crises in life, human beings are relatively powerless. The loss is so great and the challenge is so daunting that a family or couple may recognize that they will not be able to resolve the crisis. In light of these overwhelming disasters that we are sometimes forced to confront, we must learn to simply, "Let go, let God."

12—*Strong families and happy couples are prepared in advance for the challenges in life*. The best preparation we know of is to grow and nurture healthy couple and family relationships. Our love for each other is like money in the bank: If we have kept our relational accounts in order, we will be able to weather life's difficult storms by helping each other. As parents, nurturing the couple relationship as well as the family relationship becomes a model for the children to follow as they grow up in the family. Parent strategies include caring for one another in the family and commitment toward family members, especially in difficult times. Modeling behaviors strengthens couple and family bonds in both challenging *and* calm times, and are examples that children can draw from to prepare them for handling challenges in their own adult relationships.

13—*Strong families and happy couples know how to laugh and they know how to cry.* An observation of strong families is that they are fun-loving. Couples and families who enjoy life together enjoy a good laugh. They don't laugh *at* each other or at other people. Putdowns and sarcasm are not demonstrations of a person's good sense of humor; rather, they are evidence of anger and bitterness. People in healthy relationships laugh *with* each other about life's crazy twists and turns. And they are not afraid of tears, which cleanse the body of stress-related biochemicals, giving a person a feeling of genuine relief. Women who say they just had "a good cry" know what they are talking about.

14—*Strong families and happy couples do not blame others for their fate.* They do not react to crises as victims. They don't spend their time in retrospect, saying, "If only he/she had done this or tried that . . ." Instead, they work with others to build a more satisfying world for all by taking responsibility for their own actions.

15—Strong families and happy couples take life's challenges one day at a time. One woman who was in very desperate circumstances after her daughter died said that for a while, she literally took life one minute at a time. "It was hard even to breathe. I was so broken." Today, with the help of her husband—who also needed her love and support—and the help of countless other loved ones and friends, she is healthy, happy and alive.

16—Strong families and happy couples realize that suffering can be a catalyst for positive growth. Several years after her daughter died, this same woman looked back and saw quite clearly that the crisis of her daughter's death was actually a turning point in the life of the couple and the family. Crisis, by definition, is a turning point. In her case, the loss of her child led to growth and change in her life. Her marriage was strengthened as she and her husband focused on helping each other survive the death. She found new purpose in life as she subsequently went back to school and became a nurse, working with young people who have medical conditions similar to those her daughter had. The couple—whose marriage had been drawing apart—was brought back together during their daughter's illness. Once again they became best friends and were very connected to each other emotionally.

17—Strong families and happy couples identify spiritually with the grand procession of life. Strong couples and families are well aware that as individuals, we are very small, really quite insignificant, in the grand scheme of things. But we are all connected—the past, the present and the future—to something much bigger and more important: to life itself. Feeling small as we look into the Grand Canyon and see layers of rock that date back hundreds of millions of years can actually be quite satisfying and soothing to think about. We are but a drop of water in the ocean of life.

Educational Opportunities for Couples and Families

One of the best ways to learn about strong marriages is to spend time with happy couples. So, choose your friends carefully and double-up on dates with couples you respect and admire. Go out together for dinner or a movie. Invite them over to your home. Do something active outdoors with the couple and their kids.

By watching how they interact you can learn a great deal about creating strengths in your own relationship and family. Of course, you can also learn a lot about *what not to do* from unhappy couples, but frankly, you'll learn a lot more important things from the happy couples. Unhappiness in some ways can be infectious, and, likewise, the happiness couples display toward each other can also rub off on you. So, it's in your best interest to spend time with partners who clearly love and care for each other. We're not saying that you should shun couple friends who are having difficulties in life, but we are saying that you should make sure that you spend a good amount of time with couples who clearly love and honor each other and who can teach you how to be happy, also.

There are countless resources in the library and on the Internet that can help couples learn how to grow together. There are so many, in fact, that it would be truly impossible to list them all here. If you find this hard to believe, go online and visit Google. Type in "couple relationships" and over 9,000,000 sources are retrieved. Google "marriage" and over 164,000,000 come up. And Google "parenting" and over 70,000,000 sources are listed.

No, we aren't about to review every book in the library and resource listed on the Internet focusing on marriage and couple relationships. And we need to state very carefully that some of these resources are a lot better than others—searches on the Internet can find many good things and many worthless things, and, clearly, not all the books in the library are worth reading. So, pick your reading material very carefully.

However, we do have a few favorites we will cite here: Dr. David H. Olson and his colleagues in Minnesota have written an excellent book on couple relationships entitled *The Couple Checkup*. The idea is that we take our cars in for a tune-up regularly, and marital relationships also need looking at on occasion. Olson's work over more than three decades has reached literally millions of people around the world.

And, a useful Internet-based resource is the University of Nebraska–Lincoln Extension website <*http://www.extension.unl.edu/web/ extension/strongfamilies*>. The website has many articles on developing couple and family strengths and tells about the Extension book *Family Treasures*, which has more than 60 fun activities for couples and families aimed at enhancing appreciation and affection, positive communication, commitment, enjoyable time together, spiritual well-being and shared values, and the ability to manage stress and crisis effectively.

Besides written materials, there is also a vast array of face-to-face educational opportunities for couples and families. We highly recommend participation in these kinds of activities because reading about how to strengthen relationships is *important*, but seeing how this is done with your own eyes is *essential*.

These programs and experiences are often created by nonprofit institutions and organizations, including family service agencies, religious groups, schools, colleges, government organizations, private foundations and so forth. Family life education programs such as these are usually designed for couples who are doing reasonably well in their life together and are not in severe distress or crisis. Sometimes, however, couples in crisis do attend these formal educational programs and can get some help from the family life educators and the group. Also, the couple in distress can learn about how to find individualized professional help for just them as a couple.

These activities include couple enrichment programs (for example, several two-hour meetings over a six- or eight-week period). Or an hour-long lecture at a community center, or a weekend marriage encounter program at a resort. There are many different types of programs coming from many different perspectives, including whether you view life from a religious perspective or not. To find something useful to you as a couple, ask trusted friends, colleagues and family members, and go online. Be sure to shop around, of course.

Marital and Family Therapy

It is amazing to us when we think about it, but even today many couples remain hesitant about seeing a professional when they are not getting along well. They may have fallen into the trap of believing that the situation is hopeless, but it's never hopeless. There is always something that can be done to make the situation better. Or, they may not be aware of how creative professionals can be when working to help build a strong couple relationship. Maybe they feel ashamed and stupid for being caught up in an unhappy marriage and refuse to consider going for help. Or, they might not understand deep down that anything mentionable in married life is manageable, if each partner is willing to listen, to act out of genuine love and to compromise.

One undisputable fact is that no one performs his or her own brain surgery. Likewise, many relationship issues are extraordinarily complex and difficult to resolve, and outside help is essential if the partnership is to survive. Though a couple can solve most marital problems without outside help, there are many situations in which outside ideas can be very helpful.

Also, husbands and wives often do not speak openly about their feelings with each other, and a good therapist can bring out the issues in a nonthreatening and skilled way that leads to better understanding of each other. As one husband said to his wife in therapy one evening, "I now understand what you're feeling. I wish we would have come to counseling a long time ago. I could have changed." But the problem in this particular case was that he had stubbornly refused to seek help, and by the time he did agree to go to the marital therapist, the process had turned into divorce therapy. Over the years she got so tired of being angry inside because of his stubbornness that she lost all positive feelings for him. "I don't love you anymore," she told him with the therapist as her witness. Divorce proceedings had begun and the counseling they received was to help ensure that they could both still remain good parents in spite of the fact that they would not be married to each other anymore. Even though they would not be married for the rest of their lives, there was still a good chance that they could still be *parents forever* for the good of their children. Some couples are capable of doing this, while others are not.

But no one is capable of doing his own brain surgery, and in a similar fashion, there are many relationship issues that demand a great deal of knowledge, skill and understanding that we as a couple simply do not have. Creating a happy marriage is so important that it shouldn't be completely left to amateurs.

Here are some common questions that many people have about marital and family therapy:

What happens in marital counseling? Basically, the purpose is to help couples learn to communicate with each other positively and effectively. The counselor sometimes plays the role of referee, helping the partners calm down and really listen to each other. Couples often are so upset that communication has broken down. Sometimes there never was any genuine communication. But a good counselor knows how to smooth the waters and help the couple listen well and talk clearly so that solutions are possible. There is no guarantee that this will happen, but if the pair gets together and both genuinely try to make it work, chances are good.

Is there something wrong with people who go to a professional counselor? In reply to this question, we could ask another question: Is there something wrong with a person who goes to see a doctor after a heart attack? The answer to that question is easy: Of course not. The person is just being smart.

Similarly, a couple who go to a therapist to discuss a difficult marital problem are simply aware that they need outside expertise to help them work together to deal with the challenge they face. This is a wise decision, not a sign of weakness or failure.

What if one partner is willing to go but the other is not willing? Generally speaking, it is easier to work out problems when both partners are engaged and involved in the process. Sometimes one partner simply refuses to participate or argues that, "I don't need a shrink! You're the one that's crazy! You go!" In this case, the individual who wishes to go for professional help should feel free to do so. Oftentimes the advice of the therapist can be helpful for the individual coming in for a consultation.

What about situations in which violence is possible? In some situations it is not wise to involve the other partner in the professional consultation. This is especially true in cases of domestic violence in which there is considerable risk that the violent partner will erupt and do harm to the other. One marital therapist we know told the story of a couple who came in for counseling. The husband had never really listened to the wife—he had always insisted on having his way on everything. The wife finally decided to divorce him and in the counseling session when he finally listened to her and the impending divorce proceedings became clear, he stormed out of the room. Two days later he walked into a restaurant where his wife was having lunch and shot her.

Marital and family therapy can work wonders for many relationships. In the case of domestic violence, however, the endangered spouse is advised to seek counsel from programs that specialize in dealing with family violence. Similarly, alcohol and other drug abuse problems are often best treated when the non-abusing spouse seeks aid and advice from substance abuse specialists and programs that focus on these issues.

Not all marriages can be saved. And, not all marriages should be saved.

What kind of qualifications should the professional have? Licensed marital and family therapists who are certified by the American Association for Marriage and Family Therapy (AAMFT) are specifically trained to deal with relationship problems and work directly with couples and families. Although some psychologists, psychiatrists and social workers have some additional training with couples and families, these tend to be in the minority. To learn more about AAMFT, visit its website at *<aamft.org>*.

How do you find a marital or relationship therapist? The AAMFT website has a very handy *Therapist Locator* tool. Simply put in your zip code and check how many miles you are willing to drive (5 miles, 10 miles, 25 miles, 50 miles and so forth). Or you can search by city and state, or by the last name of the therapist. The *Therapist Locator* then brings up a list of professionals, and you can learn about the qualifications of each person. Also, in most localities, marital and family therapists are listed under "Marital and Family Counseling" in the yellow pages. A person also can consult a family service agency or the United Way for suggestions. Finally, there is the traditional strategy that has enabled humans to find marriage partners down through the years—through recommendations from loved ones, relatives and friends—and this method also can work for finding a marital therapist.

What if I don't like the counselor? You probably were advised to shop around for a marriage partner and not marry the first one you find. Likewise, the first marriage and family therapist you talk with may not be the right fit for you and your partner. Make this decision together, and make it carefully.

How about the cost? Rates for marital and family therapy can vary widely, from $75 to $200 per hour with an average cost of about $100 per hour. (Remember: To have the oil changed in your car, you might be paying a rate of $65 per hour or more.) Some therapists and family service agencies offer sliding fee scales so that the service is accessible to lower-income couples and families, and some private insurance programs cover the therapy with a small co-pay. A couple visiting with the counselor about an hour a week for three months might expect to pay $1,200 at $100 per hour.

Does it work? The AAMFT, which is the professional organization representing the interests of marriage and family therapists nationally, argues that research has consistently found that marriage and family therapy has proven effective for treating a wide range of mental and emotional disorders and health problems. Besides treating marital distress and conflict, marital and family therapists also treat adolescent drug abuse, depression, alcoholism, obesity and dementia in the elderly. A research team in the mid-1990s led by Bill Doherty at the University of Minnesota concluded that marital and family therapy is a rather cost-effective and efficient approach to dealing with a range of emotional and relationship problems in individuals, couples and families.

Similarly, a 2010 study by Andrew Christensen at UCLA and other colleagues around the U.S. compared traditional and nontraditional approaches to marital and family therapy for troubled married couples and found substantial positive effects as a result of the therapy. These positive effects proved true even for seriously and chronically distressed couples. However, the researchers also found that going to a therapist is no guarantee the marriage will be saved. Within two years, more than 25% of the couples in the study ended up separated or divorced.

At the risk of sounding repetitious, it is very important to be proactive in regard to marriage problems: When things aren't going right, don't be afraid to talk about the situation with your partner and work together toward a solution. Don't wait until it's too late. These problems just don't fix themselves.

All Things Considered

Getting connected and staying connected is a lifelong process for loving couples. It is also something that needs to happen *every day* of the couple's life together. Couples cannot afford to back-burner their relationship or put it on hold. They cannot afford to borrow excessive time from the relationship so they can succeed in their careers or as parents. The couple relationship is the foundation of the family and, indeed, the foundation for each individual's long-term happiness in life.

Remember: If you are successful in creating together a happy partnership, you will be married longer than you will have a job in life; and you will be married longer than you will have children living with you at home.

Many people realize only too late how easy it is for a loving relationship to slip through their fingers. Then they find themselves starting over with a new partner and a new series of challenges to face. For this reason, it is important to choose one's mate very, very carefully. Don't dive in. Think it through.

And, when you both are in agreement that it is the time to seal your partnership formally, it is essential that both individuals strive each day to make the bond a strong and loving bond.

This is done by paying attention to the fundamental strengths of a loving relationship:

- Expressing *appreciation and affection* for each other every day.
- Developing *positive communication* patterns—open and honest communication without being hurtful toward each other.
- Making a *commitment* to the relationship through thick and thin, and not falling into the trap of believing that the grass will be automatically greener in another relationship.
- Making sure that the couple has *enjoyable time together*, each and every day.
- Developing together a sense of *spiritual well-being and shared values.*
- And *managing stress and crisis in life effectively.*

And finally, back to our original question: *Where do we go from here?*

If we are wise and skillful in our interactions with each other, as a couple we will continue on through life together and the bond of love will grow even stronger. We will continue to enjoy each other's company—genuinely liking to spend time together—and we will look forward to a future that will satisfy our very human needs for love, affection and someone who genuinely cares about us.

We will have succeeded in the lifelong and essential process of getting connected and staying connected.

Short Stories from Real People

My husband had always been a member of a church. Even when he was a small boy and his parents were divorced, he went to church with a neighbor friend. Attending church, serving on boards and giving money for missions are all good things. But until we married and began to work on our faith together, my husband had never felt spirituality.

Now, many years later we have a weeklong vacation in the mountains in the summer and hike and just enjoy nature. For us, this strengthens our faith to do the work in our church. Spirituality is not confined to denomination or a building. It is in everything we see, everything we say, everything we touch. Our couple relationship grew so much closer once we discovered our couple spirituality.

Many times we have seen a family run into financial hardship as the result of expenses from some major medical event. The caring community becomes an extension of this family when they are ready to accept support. The community takes pride in whatever help they can provide; they take the family "under their wing" so to speak, helping in any way needed. This gives the family time to regroup, to appreciate what is going right, and to learn how to depend on others in times of need. It can become a win-win situation.

Expecting participation in family life was fairly easy as our children were young, but when they became teens, we really had to guard our family times. Sunday evening and breakfast became family time with everyone present. As parents, we had to make an effort to guard against outside meetings so we would be there for our children. If we, as role models, didn't think family time was important, why should they? Eating the right foods, and getting exercise and plenty of sleep were things that kept our family healthy and connected. We used mealtimes and exercise as a communication tool but also to keep our bodies healthy. My daughter's favorite activity is still a walk around the park when she visits.

Our family nearly fell apart when our son, Jason, was in an accident and spent months in the hospital. He now has disabilities that take lots of time for me, as the mom. Over this time our family started to disconnect. My husband and I were trying to do the normal things and still be at the hospital with our son. We lived in separate worlds to get everything done. The other two kids were mostly on their own, which was not always the best situation. We were failing as a family, big-time. Finally, a good friend told us about a behavioral health clinic that helps families work through their problems. We did go, all of us. It was the best thing we could have done! We all had a chance to explain what we were feeling. The therapist helped us "get on the same page." We just needed someone to listen to each of us; something we weren't doing ourselves. Now we all help take care of Jason and we are all proud to be able to help him. The clinic got all of us doing a fun event a week, so we could enjoy each other, laugh and most important, be together. What a difference finally asking for help made for our family!

Discussion Questions

1. Why do people sometimes find it difficult to *look for the good* when hard times are upon them? Give examples of how you, as a couple or a family, find ways to think positive.
2. What makes some couples or families survive turbulent times, while others seem to break under the pressure and eventually fall apart? Give an example from your own experience.
3. What can your family do to prepare for times of trial so you can handle it together, rather than letting family members fall away, contributing no support?
4. What role do you as parents play in guiding your children's management of stress and crisis?
5. How can being flexible as a family or couple be effective during a difficult time? Can you think of an example you have observed?

6. Communication is key to tackling difficult situations. What is communication like in your home? Are there ways you can work together to improve communication?

Tips for Strengthening Your Relationship

1. A positive attitude is critical for the sake of yourself, your spouse and your family. Identify five positives for each negative you see in your life.
2. Find ways to see the good in any unpleasant situation.
3. Spend time together as a couple or family doing something that brings out the humor in the relationship . . . maybe a movie, sharing jokes, watching funny TV shows, or best of all, sitting around the family table sharing funny stories and experiences.
4. Keep your problems in perspective; don't let a stressful situation consume your family or couple life.
5. Professional help is sometimes needed. Don't ignore it!
6. Volunteer to help those less fortunate than yourself. This is especially beneficial when done as a couple or family, rather than individually.
7. Don't underestimate the value of conversation, blended with focused listening, to make your family relationship and your couple relationship stronger.

READINGS FOR GREATER UNDERSTANDING

The ideas represented in this book are based on the best research and theory available in the field of family studies today. Readers interested in digging deeper are encouraged to study sources listed below. And, a search on the Internet will uncover countless other useful materials.

Chapter 1

DeFrain, J., & Asay, S. M. (2007). *Strong families around the world: Strengths-based research and perspectives.* London and New York: Routledge, Taylor & Francis Group.

DeFrain, J., Brand, G., Fenton, A., Friesen, J., Hanna, J., Lodl, K., Nelson, M., Sherry, L., & UNL For Families Writing Team. (2006). *Family treasures: Creating strong families.* New York, Lincoln, and Shanghai, China: iUniverse.

Olson, D. H., DeFrain, J., & Skogrand, L. (2011). *Marriages and families: Intimacy, diversity, and strengths* (7th ed.). New York: McGraw-Hill Higher Education.

Waite, L., & Gallagher, M. (2000). *The case for marriage: Why married people are happier, healthier, and better off financially.* New York: Doubleday.

Chapter 2

Duvall, E. M., & Miller, B. C. (1985). *Marriage and family development* (6th ed.). New York: Harper & Row.

Hunt, S. (2005). The life course: A sociological introduction. New York: Palgrave MacMillan.

Owens, T. J., & Suitor, J. J. (Eds.). (2007). *Advances in life course research: Vol. 12, Interpersonal relations across the life course.* Amsterdam: Elsevier.

Chapter 3

Olson, D. H., DeFrain, J., & Skogrand, L. (2011). *Marriages and families: Intimacy, diversity, and strengths* (7th ed.). New York: McGraw-Hill Higher Education.

Chapter 4

DeFrain, J., Brand, G., Fenton, A., Friesen, J., Hanna, J., Lodl, K., Nelson, M., Sherry, L., & UNL For Families Writing Team. (2007*). Family treasures: Creating strong families.* New York, Lincoln, and Shanghai, China: iUniverse. Outlines 35 years of family strengths research at the University of Nebraska–Lincoln, University of Alabama at Tuscaloosa, and allied universities across the country and around the world. The highlight of the book is the collection of more than 60 activities for strengthening couple and family relationships, designed specifically for enhancing each of the six major family strengths.

DeFrain, J., Brand, G., Fenton, A., Friesen, J., Hanna, J., Lodl, K., Nelson, M., Sherry, L., & UNL For Families Writing Team. (2007*). Creating strong families: Family treasures supplement.* Lincoln, NE: University of Nebraska-Lincoln Extension. This CD and DVD collection is available from the UNL for Families website *<unlforfamilies.unl.edu>*. The CD *Family Treasures Supplement* includes resources for educators, a video viewing guide, and resources for families. The DVD *Family Treasures Video Supplement* includes the Family Strengths Model and four activities featuring families enjoying their time together: The Best Summer Ever, Family Bingo Game, Take a Stand, and the Balloon Activity.

Olson, D. H., DeFrain, J., & Skogrand, L. (2011). *Marriages and families: Intimacy, diversity, and strengths* (7th ed.). New York: McGraw-Hill Higher Education.

Chapter 5

Gottman, J. M. (2001). *The relationship cure.* New York: Three Rivers Press. How to develop emotional connections and a stronger relationship.

Markman, H. J., Stanley, S. M., & Blumberg, S. L. (2001). *Fighting for your marriage*. San Francisco: Jossey Bass. Focuses on building positive communication skills.

Olson, D. H., DeFrain, J., & Skogrand, L. (2011). *Marriages and families: Intimacy, diversity, and strengths* (7th ed.). New York: McGraw-Hill Higher Education.

Olson, D. H., Olson-Sigg, A., & Larson, P. (2008). *The couple checkup*. Nashville, TN: Thomas Nelson.

Chapter 6

Alberti, R. E., & Emmons, M. (2001). *Your perfect right: Assertiveness and equality in your life*. Atascadero, CA: Impact.

American Association for Marital and Family Therapy (AAMFT). The premier professional organization for marital and family therapists and their clients. Visit the AAMFT website to learn more about relationship and mental health counseling, including information on family problems and how to find a family therapist in your vicinity. *www.aamft.org*

Borcherdt, B. (2000). *You can control your anger! 21 ways to do it*. Sarasota, FL: Professional Resource Press.

Lerner, H. G. (2005). *The dance of anger: A woman's guide to changing the patterns of intimate relationships*. New York: Perennial Currents.

Chapter 7

Davis, K. E. (2004). *Love's many faces apprehended*. Washington, DC: American Psychological Association.

Olson, D. H., Olson-Sigg, A., & Larson, P. (2008). *The couple checkup*. Nashville, TN: Thomas Nelson.

Pines, A. M. (1998). *Romantic jealousy: Causes, symptoms, cures*. New York: Routledge, Taylor & Francis Group.

Sternberg, R. J., & Barnes, M. (Eds.). (1988). *The psychology of love*. New Haven, CT: Yale University Press.

Chapter 8

Lindsey, L. L. (2011). Gender roles: A sociological perspective (5th ed.). Upper Saddle River, NJ: Pearson Prentice Hall.

Mead, M. (1935). *Sex and temperament in three primitive societies.* New York: Morrow/Quill.

Olson, D. H., Olson-Sigg, A., & Larson, P. (2008). *The couple checkup.* Nashville, TN: Thomas Nelson.

Chapter 9

Alberti, R., & Emmons, M. (2008). *Your perfect right: Assertiveness and equality in your life and relationships* (9th ed.). Atascadero, CA: Impact.

Cherlin, A. (2009). *The marriage-go-round: The state of marriage and family in America today.* Clashing values have caused more partnering and re-partnering in the U.S. than elsewhere in the world, Cherlin argues. The reason, in part, is that Americans value both marriage and individualism.

Dalla, R., DeFrain, J., Johnson, J., & Abbott, D. (2008). *Strengths and challenges of new immigrant families: Implications for research, education, policy, and service.* Landover, Maryland: Lexington Books, Rowman & Littlefield.

Massey, D. S. (2008). *New faces in new places: The changing geography of American immigration.* New York: Russell Sage Foundation.

Hennon, C. B., & Wilson, S. M. (Eds.). (2008). *Families in a global context.* London: Routledge, Taylor & Francis Group. How are families the same or different around the world? An in-depth analysis of family life in 17 countries.

Keirsey, D., & Bates, M. (1984). *Please understand me: Character and temperament types.* Del Mar, CA: Prometheus Nemesis. Outlines the four temperaments and 16 types that have been copied and imitated by other authors for more than 40 years. Includes the Keirsey Temperament Sorter.

Keirsey, D. (1998). *Please understand me II: Temperament, character, intelligence* (1st ed.). Del Mar, CA: Prometheus Nemesis.

Olson, D. H., Olson-Sigg, A., & Larson, P. J. (2008). *The couple checkup.* Nashville, TN: Thomas Nelson. Based on a survey of 50,000 couples, the book is an effort to help couples find the strengths in their relationship and build on these strengths.

Tannen, D. (2003). *Communication matters.* Course one: *He said / she said, women, men and language* [sound recording]. Prince Frederick, MD: Recorded Books. Deborah Tannen has focused our attention on the differences between male and female communication styles and how these differences affect our relationships with each other.

Chapman, G. (2008). *The heart of the five love languages: The secret to love that lasts.* Chicago: Northfield Publishing.

Chapter 10

Fox, M., et al. (2009). *Survive strive thrive: Keys to healthy family living.* MP89. Lincoln, NE: University of Nebraska–Lincoln Extension. Website: *www.ianrpubs.unl.edu.* A 15-unit curriculum that takes teens and adults from day-to-day surviving through thriving. Includes sections on money management, goal setting, stress management, communication, time management, coping skills, making good decisions, and so forth.

Garman, E. T., & Forgue, R. (2010). *Personal finance* (10th ed.). Mason, OH: South-Western Cengage Learning. An excellent college-level text. Very useful.

Holland, M. A., Manning, L., Nisley, A., & Scholtz, D. (2008). *Making cents of it.* Lincoln, NE: University of Nebraska–Lincoln. Website: *www.ianrpubs.unl.edu.* Helping younger children learn about money management. An educator guide for grades two and three.

Rich, J. (2003). *The couple's guide to love and money.* Oakland, CA: New Harbinger. A good place to start.

Schroeder, D. (2007). *Preventing the credit card blues at 22* (CD8). A computer curriculum targeted to high school students to help them to make good decisions about credit card use. Lincoln, NE: University of Nebraska–Lincoln Extension. Website: *www.ianrpubs.unl.edu.*

Chapter 11

Gottman, J. M. (2007). *And baby makes three: The six-step plan for preserving marital intimacy and rekindling romance after baby arrives.* New York: Crown.

Smith, J. A. (2009). *The daddy shift: How stay-at-home dads, breadwinning moms, and shared parenting are transforming the American family.* Boston: Beacon Press. What happens when dads stay home? What do stay-at-home fathers struggle with and what do they rejoice in?

Chapter 12

American Association for Marriage and Family Therapy. (2010). *Infidelity.* Website: aamft.org.

Olson, D. H., Olson-Sigg, A., & Larson, P. J. (2007). *The couple checkup.* Nashville, TN: Thomas Nelson. Based on a national survey of 50,000 couples; for dating, engaged, and married couples. A strengths-based approach to improving the relationship.

Pittman, F. (1993). *Private lies: Infidelity and the betrayal of intimacy.* New York: Norton. A very wise family therapist shares his experience working with couples who are dealing with an extramarital affair.

Chapter 13

Boss, P. (2002). *Family stress management: A contextual approach.* Thousand Oaks, CA: Sage. Why do some families survive stressful situations while others fall apart?

Boss, P. (2006). *Loss, trauma, and resilience: Therapeutic work with ambiguous loss.* Dunmore, PA: Norton. Making sense of tragedies that are difficult to understand.

Cullington, D. (2008). *Breaking up blues.* New York: Routledge, Taylor & Francis Group. Surviving the loss of a relationship.

Scott, M. J. (2007). *Moving on after trauma.* New York: Routledge, Taylor & Francis Group.

Skogrand, L., DeFrain, N., DeFrain, J., & Jones, J. (2007). *Surviving and transcending a traumatic childhood: The dark thread.* New York: Haworth.

Chapter 14

Bray, J. H., & Kelly, J. (1998). *Stepfamilies—Love, marriage, and parenting in the first decade.* New York: Broadway Books.

Deal, R. L., & Olson, D. H. (2010). *The remarriage checkup.* Bloomington, MN: Bethany House Publishers.

Gabe, G., & Lipman-Blumen, J. (2004). *Step wars—Overcoming the perils of making peace in adult stepfamilies.* New York: St. Martin's Press.

Kansas State University Research and Extension. (2010). *Stepping stones for stepfamilies—A program to strengthen stepfamilies.* Website: *http://www.ksre.ksu.edu/families/-DesktopDefault.aspx?tabid=39*

Lutz, E. (1998). *The complete idiot's guide to stepparenting.* New York: Alpha Books.

National Stepfamily Resource Center. (2010). Welcome to The National Stepfamily Resource Center. Website: *http://www.stepfamilies.info/about.php*

Parrott, Les, & Parrott, Leslie. (2001). *Saving your second marriage before it starts.* Grand Rapids, MI: Zondervan.

Chapter 15

American Association for Marriage and Family Therapy. (2011). Excellent information on the process of marriage and family therapy, how to find a therapist, and discussions of various problems that couples face. Website: *www.aamft.org/iMIS15/AAMFT/*

American Family Strengths Inventory (AFSI). (2011). An at-home, free assessment of couple and family strengths. Take the inventory with your partner and other family members and plan how to enhance your strengths and improve areas of potential growth in your relationships. Website: *http://www.ianrpubs.unl.edu/-epublic/live/g1881/build/g1881.pdf*

Doherty, W. J. (2000). *Take back your kids.* Notre Dame, IN: Sorin Books.

Gurman, A. (2008). *Clinical handbook of couple therapy* (4th ed.). New York: Guilford Press.

Hecker, L. L., & Wetchler, J. L. (Eds.). *An introduction to marriage and family therapy.* London: Routledge, Taylor & Francis Group. Insight and analysis from 20 experts.

Kansas State University at Manhattan. (2011). Useful resources for couples and families. Website: *http://www.oznet.ksu.edu/DesktopDefault.aspx?tabid=22*

National Council on Family Relations. (2011). NCFR was founded in 1938 and is the oldest multidisciplinary and nonpartisan professional organization focused solely on family research, practice, and education. Website: *http://www.ncfr.org*

Olson, D. H., Olson-Sigg, A., & Larson, P. J. (2008). *The couple checkup: Finding your relationship strengths.* Nashville, TN: Thomas Nelson.

University of Missouri at Columbia Extension. (2011). Educational materials for couples and families. Website: *http://www.extension. missouri.edu/main/family/-index.shtml*

University of Nebraska–Lincoln. (2011). Educational materials for strengthening couple and family relationships. Website: *http://www. ianrpubs.unl.edu/-epublic/pages/index.jsp*

References

Chapter 1

DeFrain, J., & Asay, S. M. (2007). *Strong families around the world: Strengths-based research and perspectives*. London and New York: Routledge, Taylor & Francis Group.

Olson, D. H., DeFrain, J., & Skogrand, L. (2011). *Marriages and families: Intimacy, diversity, and strengths* (7th ed.). New York: McGraw-Hill Higher Education.

Waite, L., & Gallagher, M. (2000). *The case for marriage: Why married people are happier, healthier, and better off financially*. New York: Doubleday.

Chapter 2

Duvall, E. M., & Miller, B. C. (1985). *Marriage and family development* (6th ed.). New York: Harper & Row.

Hunt, S. (2005). The life course: A sociological introduction. New York: Palgrave MacMillan.

Owens, T. J., & Suitor, J. J. (Eds.). (2007). *Advances in life course research: Vol. 12, Interpersonal relations across the life course*. Amsterdam: Elsevier.

Chapter 3

Connell, G., Mitten, T., & Bumberry, W. M. (1999). *Reshaping family relationships: The symbolic therapy of Carl Whitaker*. London and New York: Routledge, Taylor & Francis Group.

Goldenberg, H., & Goldenberg, I. (2007). *Family therapy: An overview*. Belmont, CA: Brooks/Cole.

Murstein, B. I. (1987). A classification and extension of the SVR theory of dyadic pairing. *Journal of Marriage and the Family, 42,* 777-792.

Olson, D. H., DeFrain, J., & Skogrand, L. (2011). *Marriages and families: Intimacy, diversity, and strengths* (7th ed.). New York: McGraw-Hill Higher Education.

Olson, D. H., Olson-Sigg, A., & Larson, P. (2008). *The couple checkup*. Nashville, TN: Thomas Nelson.

Reiss, I. L., & Lee, G. R. (1988). *Family systems in America* (4th ed.). New York: Holt, Rinehart & Winston.

Winch, R. F. (1958). *Mate selection: A study of complementary needs*. New York: Harper.

Chapter 4

DeFrain, J., Brand, G., Fenton, A., Friesen, J., Hanna, J., Lodl, K., Nelson, M., Sherry, L., & UNL For Families Writing Team. (2007*). Family treasures: Creating strong families*. New York, Lincoln, and Shanghai, China: iUniverse.

DeFrain, J., & Asay, S. (Eds.). (2007). *Strong families around the world*: *Strengths-based research and perspectives*. London and New York: Haworth Press/Taylor & Francis.

Chapter 5

Gottman, J. M. (2001). *The relationship cure*. New York: Three Rivers Press.

Markman, H. J., Stanley, S. M., & Blumberg, S. L. (2001). *Fighting for your marriage*. San Francisco: Jossey Bass.

Olson, D. H., DeFrain, J., & Skogrand, L. (2011). *Marriages and families: Intimacy, diversity, and strengths* (7th ed.). New York: McGraw-Hill Higher Education.

Olson, D. H., Olson-Sigg, A., & Larson, P. (2008). *The couple checkup*. Nashville, TN: Thomas Nelson.

Chapter 6

Alberti, R. E., & Emmons, M. (2001). *Your perfect right: Assertiveness and equality in your life*. Atascadero, CA: Impact.

Borcherdt, B. (2000). *You can control your anger! 21 ways to do it*. Sarasota, FL: Professional Resource Press.

Lerner, H. G. (2005). *The dance of anger: A woman's guide to changing the patterns of intimate relationships.* New York: Perennial Currents.

Chapter 7

Davis, K. E. (2004). *Love's many faces apprehended.* Washington, DC: American Psychological Association.

Levy, K., Kelly, K. M., & Jack, E. L. (2006). Sex differences in jealousy: A matter of evolution or attachment theory? In M. Mikulincer & G. S. Goodman (Eds.), *Dynamics of romantic love: Attachment, caregiving, and sex* (pp. 128-145). New York: Guilford.

Marelich, W. D., Gaines, S. O., & Banzet, M. R. (2003). Commitment, insecurity and arousability: Testing a transactional model of jealousy. *Representative Research in Social Psychology, 27,* 23-31.

Pines, A. M. (1998). *Romantic jealousy: Causes, symptoms, cures.* New York: Routledge.

Puente, S., & Cohen, D. (2003). Jealousy and the meaning (or nonmeaning) of violence. *Personality & Social Psychology Bulletin, 29*(4), 449-460.

Sternberg, R. J., & Barnes, M. (Eds.). (1988). *The psychology of love.* New Haven, CT: Yale University Press.

Chapter 8

Buss, D. M., Shackelford, T. K., Kirkpatrick, L. A., & Larsen, R. J. (2001). A half century of mate preferences: The cultural evolution of values. *Journal of Marriage and the Family, 63,* 491-503.

Gallup poll. (1996). *Gender and society: Status and stereotypes.* Princeton, NJ: The Gallup Organization.

Gallup poll. (2001, February 21). *Americans see women as emotional and affectionate, men as more aggressive.* Princeton, NJ: The Gallup Organization.

Geggie, J., DeFrain, J., Hitchcock, S., & Silberberg, S. (2000). *Family strengths research project.* A national project funded by the Commonwealth Department of Family and Community Services under the Stronger Families and Community Strategy. Callaghan, NSW, Australia: University of Newcastle Family Action Centre.

Herbst, P. G. (1952). The measurement of family relationships. *Human Relations, 5,* 3-35.

Mead, M. (1935). *Sex and temperament in three primitive societies.* New York: Morrow/Quill.

Meier, J. S., McNaughton-Cassill, M., & Lynch, M. (2006). The management of household and childcare tasks and relationship satisfaction in parenting couples. *Marriage and Family Review, 40,* 61-88.

Olson, D. H., Olson-Sigg, A., & Larson, P. (2008). *The couple checkup.* Nashville, TN: Thomas Nelson.

Parsons, T. (1955). The American family: Its relations to personality and the social structure. In T. Parsons & R. F. Bales (Eds.), *Family socialization and interaction process* (pp. 3-21). Glencoe, IL: Free Press.

Parsons, T. (1965). The normal American family. In S. M. Farber, P. Mustacchi, & R. H. L. Wilson (Eds.), *Man and civilization: The family's search for survival* (pp. 31-50). New York: McGraw-Hill.

Chapter 9

Alberti, R., & Emmons, M. (2008). *Your perfect right: Assertiveness and equality in your life and relationships* (9th ed.). Atascadero, CA: Impact.

Chapman, G. (2008). *The heart of the five love languages: The secret to love that lasts.* Northfield, MN: Northfield Publishing.

Cherlin, A. (2009). *The marriage-go-round: The state of marriage and family in America today.*

Dalla, R., DeFrain, J., Johnson, J., & Abbott, D. (2008). *Strengths and challenges of new immigrant families: Implications for research, education, policy, and service.* Landover, Maryland: Lexington Books, Rowman & Littlefield.

Massey, D. S. (2008). *New faces in new places: The changing geography of American immigration.* New York: Russell Sage Foundation.

Hennon, C. B., & Wilson, S. M. (Eds.). (2008). *Families in a global context.* London and New York: Routledge, Taylor & Francis Group.

Keirsey, D., & Bates, M. (1984). *Please understand me: Character and temperament types.* Del Mar, CA: Prometheus Nemesis.

Keirsey, D. (1998). *Please understand me II: Temperament, character, intelligence* (1st ed.). Del Mar, CA: Prometheus Nemesis.

Tannen, D. (2003). *Communication Matters.* Course one: *He said / she said, women, men and language* [sound recording]. Prince Frederick, MD: Recorded Books.

Chapter 10

Garman, E. T., & Forgue, R. (2010). *Personal finance* (10ᵗʰ ed.). Mason, OH: South-Western Cengage Learning.

Hendricks, E. (2005). *Credit scores and credit reports* (pp. 20-21). Cabin John, MD: Privacy Times, Inc.

National Curriculum and Training Institute, Inc. (2011). *Real colors.* Website: *http://www.realcolors.org/page_6.php*

Olson, D. H., Olson-Sigg, A., & Larson, P. (2008). *The couple checkup.* Nashville, TN: Thomas Nelson.

Orman, S. (2011). *Five ways to improve your credit score. Money matters with Suze Orman: A yearlong series on making the most of your money.* Website: *http://biz.yahoo.com/pfg/e35score/art021.html*

Rich, J. (2003). *The couple's guide to love and money.* Oakland, CA: New Harbinger.

Sahadi, J. (2005). Why being good can be bad for your credit. *Money,* November, p. 50.

Chapter 11

Gottman, J. M. (2007). *And baby makes three: The six-step plan for preserving marital intimacy and rekindling romance after baby arrives.* New York: Crown.

Smith, J. A. (2009). *The daddy shift: How stay-at-home dads, breadwinning moms, and shared parenting are transforming the American family.* Boston: Beacon Press.

Woolman, L. (January 1, 2006). How children serve to deepen a couple's marital bond: A qualitative study of great marriages. *ETD collection for University of Nebraska–Lincoln.* Paper AAI3237487. Website: *http://digitalcommons.unl.edu/-dissertations/AAI3237487*

Chapter 12

Brown, E. (2000). *Patterns of infidelity and their treatment.* London: Brunner/Mazel.

Pittman, F. (1993). *Private lies: Infidelity and the betrayal of intimacy.* New York: Norton.

Chapter 13

Hill, R. (1958). Generic features of families under stress. *Social Casework, 49,* 139-150.

Olson, D. H., McCubbin, H. I., Barnes, H., Larsen, A., Muxen, M., & Wilson, M. (1989). *Families: What makes them work?* (2nd ed.). Los Angeles, CA: Sage.

Chapter 14

Bray, J. H., & Kelly, J. (1998). *Stepfamilies—Love, marriage, and parenting in the first decade.* New York: Broadway Books.

Carter, B., & McGoldrick, M. (Eds.). (2005). *The expanded family life cycle: Individual, family, and social perspectives.* New York: Pearson Allyn & Bacon.

Deal, R. L., & Olson, D. H. (2010). *The remarriage checkup.* Bloomington, MN: Bethany House Publishers.

Doherty, W. J. (1997). *The intentional family—Simple rituals to strengthen family ties.* New York: Quill / Harper Collins.

Lutz, E. (1998). *The complete idiot's guide to stepparenting.* New York: Alpha Books.

Meridian Education Corporation. (1997). *Invasion of the Step People.* Bloomington, IL: Meridian Education Corporation.

National Healthy Marriage Resource Center. (2009). Stepfamilies in the United States: A fact sheet. Website: *http://www.healthymarriageinfo.org/docs/-stepfamiliesintheus.pdf*

National Stepfamily Resource Center. (2010). Stepfamily fact sheet. Website: *http://www.stepfamilies.info/faqs/factsheet.php*

Olson, D. H., DeFrain, J. D., & Skogrand, L. (2011). *Marriages and families: Intimacy, diversity, and strengths* (7th ed.). New York: McGraw-Hill Higher Education.

Parrott, Les, & Parrott, Leslie. (2001). *Saving your second marriage before it starts.* Grand Rapids, MI: Zondervan.

Stepfamily Foundation. (2009). Statistics. Website: *http://www.stepfamily. org/-statistics.html*

U.S. Census Bureau. (2000b). Census 2000 brief: Overview of race and Hispanic origin, 2000. Website: *http://www.census.gov*

Chapter 15

American Association for Marriage and Family Therapy. (2009). Frequently asked questions on marriage and family therapy. Website: *http:///www. aamft.org/-faqs/index_nm.asp*

Christensen, A., Atkins, D. C., Baucom, B., & Yi, J. (2010). Marital status and satisfaction five years following a randomized clinical trial comparing traditional versus integrative behavioral couple therapy. *Journal of Consulting and Clinical Psychology, 78*(2), 225-235.

Doherty, W. S., & Simmons, D. S. (1996). Clinical practice patterns of marriage and family therapists: A national survey of therapists and their clients. *Journal of Marital and Family Therapy, 22*, 9-25.

Tulane, S., Skogrand, L., & DeFrain, J. (2011). Couples in great marriages who considered divorcing. Logan, UT: Department of Family, Consumer and Human Development, Utah State University. For more information, contact Dr. Linda Skogrand, Associate Professor and Extension Specialist: *linda.skogrand@usu.edu.*

INDEX

Made in the USA
Middletown, DE
13 January 2020